W0115685

JOHN
DEWEY

Compiled and Edited by

Southern Illinois University Press
Feffer & Simons, Inc.

A Checklist
of Translations,
1900–1967

Jo Ann Boydston

with

Robert L. Andresen

Carbondale and Edwardsville
London and Amsterdam

Preface

GENERAL

John Dewey's published works were regularly abstracted and reviewed in both the *Revue philosophique* and the *Revue de métaphysique et de morale*, beginning in 1882 when his first article appeared. However, no translations of any of his works appeared until eighteen years later. This Checklist, therefore, begins with the year of that first translation, 1900. By making 1967 the last full year covered by the Checklist, we have added a follow-up period of fifteen years to Dewey's long publishing career of seventy years (1882-1952). The primary purpose of a checklist of translations is to provide a framework for information available now and in the future. The task of searching for new translations and of completing data on known translations is continuous. We earnestly solicit the co-operation of interested librarians and Dewey scholars for the constant additions and corrections needed in a work of this kind. Such assistance will be as important in future revisions as it has been in the compilation of this Checklist.

NEED FOR CHECKLIST

Since the beginning of the twentieth century, John Dewey has been the best known and most influential educator in the world. His work as a philosopher has also had continuing impact on scholars everywhere. Even though many philosophers, educators, and social scientists in other countries became acquainted with Dewey by reading his work in English, any assessment of his influence abroad must consider translations available to these scholars in their own language. Writings published in the native language naturally attract more readers and exercise more influence among scholars. The reverse is also true--a certain climate of receptivity probably exists before a translator prepares his work and before a publisher undertakes to make it available.

For each language and culture, the information in this Checklist is valuable for various kinds of studies. For instance, why has Italy shown such a broad and continuing interest in Dewey scholarship as evidenced by the constantly growing number of Italian articles on Dewey and his thought? To answer such a question, information about Italian translations of Dewey's works is indispensable. Which of Dewey's writings have been readily available to the Italian scholar in his own language? Which of Dewey's works have been considered important enough to be translated into Italian by more than one person? Which translations have been most frequently reprinted--and when? What relationship exists between social and cultural developments in a country and the choice of works translated at the time?

Across the spectrum of languages into which Dewey's works have been translated, questions of a broader nature may be posed. Which writings have been translated into the greatest number of languages? At what period in history? Even the omissions--those of Dewey's works that apparently have not yet appealed to a translator in any language--are significant. The Dewey scholar of any country should have available the complete story of the frequency and spread of translations of a given Dewey work. That *Democracy and Education* is the single work of Dewey's which has been translated more times than any other is perhaps not surprising, but the fact--gleaned from these pages-- that *Freedom and Culture* is the single Dewey work that has appeared in more different languages than any other item gives rise to questions that may initiate profitable study.

SOURCES

M. H. Thomas' *John Dewey: A Centennial Bibliography* (Chicago: University of Chicago Press, 1962) provided basic information for translations published between 1900 and 1962. A second important source was the *Index Translationum* (Paris: UNESCO, 1932-1967). Somewhat different in nature but equally important in the early stages was correspondence with national libraries in countries around the world, both in obtaining initial listings and in adding to or correcting data from other sources. A number of these libraries graciously performed many tasks of investigation and provided exhaustive listings. In the United States and

Canada, Xerox copies of card catalog listings from a
number of universities provided verifications and additions. The bibliographical publications of various
countries yielded further leads and confirming information. Publishers, as well, were helpful and consid-
erate in responding to queries about works long out of
print. Additional information came from the United
States Information Agency and the Orientalia Division
of the Reference Department of the Library of Congress.
As all these sources are listed alphabetically on
pages 93-100, the interested bibliographer may pursue
information as he desires. The list may serve also as
a guide for compilation of similar checklists of translations of the works of other authors.

CHRONOLOGICAL TABLE

Before the comprehensive listing of translations, a
table summarizes the works translated into the various
languages in the years covered. Independent translations of the same work are listed separately in the
year of their appearance. All articles and other
works published in collections are cited by original
English title.

MAIN ENTRIES

The main section of the Checklist includes translations of Dewey's articles and books arranged in alphabetical order, numbered 1-67. Under each numbered entry appear the translations in alphabetical order by
language, designated by a letter in small roman type.
In cases of multiple translations in a language, the
translations are arranged in chronological order. The
running head includes the letter of the alphabet of
Dewey's original work, the number of the item on the
page, and the page number separated from the rest of
the key by a diagonal.

COLLECTIONS

The main alphabetical listing also includes English
collections of Dewey's works if they have been translated in their entirety into another language, whether
the collection was made by Dewey himself or by an editor. The last four items in this section, 64-67, rep-
resent exceptions to the general nature of the other
items: The collections *Der Projekt-Plan, L'école et*

l'enfant, Ensayos de educación, and *Il mio credo peda-gogico: Antologia dei scritti sull'educazione* did not first appear as collections in English. However, *L'école et l'enfant* has been translated as a unit from French into other languages, and the other three are collections of a number of Dewey articles for which publishing information is most practically listed only once rather than in connection with each item included in the collection. Collections which include items by Dewey as well as by other authors do not appear as main entries; they are simply referred to in the regular bibliographical information as sources of the Dewey items.

RE-TRANSLATIONS

The next section (items 68-71) lists Dewey's writings which were first published in French and later re-translated into English. Although Dewey originally wrote these materials in English prior to their translation and publication in another language, the English manuscript has been lost. They are listed separately from the other translations because there is no original English version extant with which to compare the French translations. The student should note carefully that the English version available today is twice removed from Dewey's first writing, *i.e.*, it is an English translation from the French translation of Dewey's original English version.

UNTRANSLATED PUBLICATIONS

The third section (items 72-75) is made up of four articles published in Japanese and not yet translated into English. These are listed separately because they are not available in English. A study of the article "Some Factors in Mutual National Understanding" (57) can provide insight into the quality of the translation into Japanese. This item was the first of a series published in *Kaizō* and appeared in both Japanese and English in the same issue. The four remaining articles in the series, which have appeared only in Japanese, are listed in this section of the Checklist.

CHINESE LECTURES

The last section (items 76-154) lists Dewey's Chinese lectures, which have never appeared in English. Be-

cause Dewey's main impact on Chinese thought and history came by way of these lectures, the titles and publication information should be available to students of
Dewey. These lectures are not Dewey "publications" in
the strictest sense of the term because he delivered
the lectures orally in English and they were simultan-
eously interpreted into Chinese from the platform for
the audience. The Chinese versions were recorded from
the interpreted oral presentation at that time and
later published in newspapers and other periodicals.
Thus the Chinese form available to us today is not
only removed from Dewey's original by translation but
also by recording from the oral delivery in Chinese.

STYLE

For each main entry, publication information about
the first printed version of Dewey's work appears im-
mediately after the entry number. When revised and re-
printed versions of Dewey's work exist as a possible
basis for the translation, these are listed after the
main entry, enclosed in brackets. Book titles are in
roman capital letters and articles are in upper and
lower case roman type, enclosed in quotation marks.
Except for Dewey main entries, book titles appear in
upper and lower case italic type as do titles of periodicals. Book titles are repeated without the number,
underlined in upper and lower case roman type, as a
heading for translated "selections." Parts of books,
chapters, isolated paragraphs, and abstracted material
appear under this heading. Series titles are enclosed
in parentheses following the name of the translator or
editor. When necessary, contents of books are listed
before the lettered translation entries. Other rele-
vant explanatory information is enclosed in brackets
following the main entry and following the translation
entry.

PUNCTUATION AND SPELLING

All titles have been transliterated into the Roman
alphabet. Spelling, punctuation, and use of accent
marks of various kinds follows the usage of communica-
tions from libraries of the countries in question in
preference to sources published chiefly for English-
speaking persons. Place names are in the English form.
Surnames are listed last regardless of the practice in
the translator's native language. Chief words in se-

ries titles are capitalized. Book and article titles follow the *MLA International Bibliography Style Sheet* pattern: Only the first word in the entry or following a colon is capitalized in languages other than German and English. In German, nouns are also capitalized. In English, all important words are capitalized. However, in series titles and publishers' designations, all main words are capitalized regardless of language.

PRINTING AND EDITION

All known printings of each translation are listed, with dates and other information available. The distinction consistently made here between "edition" and "printing" follows Fredson Bowers' definition ". . . an edition comprises a particular typesetting, without regard for the number of printings made at different times from this typesetting or its plates."[1] The edition is the principal subentry and its various printings are so labeled and are indented under the edition listing. Lack of opportunity to examine the books firsthand made one deviation from the basic definition necessary: If a different publisher issued the translation, even though the translator and number of pages might seem to indicate a reprinting rather than a new edition, the item has been called a new edition. Thus, without information verifying that it is a simple reprinting, the printing has arbitrarily been labeled a new edition when a new publisher appears in the listing. Publishers' designations of "editions" which are clearly a succession of reprintings, have been ignored. Details of changes in series titles, and minor changes in total number of pages appear with the printing which incorporated the change.

CROSS REFERENCES

Cross references to other items in the main list are regularly made by the use of *"See"* with the number of

---

[1] p. ix, "Textual Principles and Procedures," *Psychology* by John Dewey (Carbondale, Illinois: Southern Illinois University Press, 1967). For a fuller description of the terms "edition" and "printing" see Fredson Bowers, *Principles of Bibliographical Description* (Princeton: Princeton University Press, 1949), pp. 379–426.

the item. This indicates a collection in which the
translated item appeared; full publication information
appears at that number. When an item includes only
two works, each is listed independently with the other
part mentioned in brackets.

LOCATION OF TRANSLATIONS

There has been no attempt to suggest where copies of
the translations are located. Much of the information
included here came from bibliographical listings rather
than from card catalogs or library correspondence; many
of the works have long been out of print, cannot be
purchased, and are not held in collections in this
country. Although it has not been possible to examine
most of the works themselves, a determined effort has
been made to check and cross-check the existence of
each translation and to verify the information by its
appearance in several different sources and by correspondence with the publisher.

SUPPLEMENTARY MATERIAL

To make this Checklist maximally useful as a reference tool, five sections (one of which precedes the
list of translations) substitute for the traditional
index: (1) a chronological listing of translations;
(2) an index of languages into which Dewey's English works
have been translated, thirty-four in all, keyed to the
numbers and letters in the list of translations; (3)
an index of names of translators, editors, and pref-
acers; (4) an index of introductions and prefaces,
many of which are article-length; and, (5) an index of
terms and names that appear in titles.

ACKNOWLEDGMENTS

This Checklist has been prepared as a subsidiary en-
terprise under the auspices of the Project known as
Co-operative Research on Dewey Publications, in the
Office of Research and Projects of the Graduate School
of Southern Illinois University. The "Dewey Project"
is primarily engaged in preparing and publishing the
collected works of John Dewey. It has been possible
to put together the present work because of the gener-
ous co-operation of numerous persons at Southern Illinois University; we are particularly grateful to

William E. Simeone, Dean of Graduate Studies and Research and Ronald G. Hansen, Co-ordinator of Research
and Projects. The staff at Morris Library continue to
support and encourage our work: Harold J. Rath, Thomas Kilpatrick, Alan M. Cohn, Hensley C. Woodbridge
(who read the MS), and many others. We are grateful
also for the contributions made by the College of Education at the University of Illinois, Champaign-Urbana,
and by Joe R. Burnett and Burton Raimer there.

The Chinese materials deserve a special mention:
The first comprehensive listing of the lectures was
made at the East-West Center at the University of Ha-
waii under the direction of Robert Clopton; much additional work was done by Barry Keenan. Mr. Keenan was
continually gracious and co-operative in assisting with
the present Checklist--transliterating from the Chinese,
correcting and verifying information about translations.
We modified Mr. Keenan's final list of the lectures for
special use here; his list will appear as an appendix
to the published translation of the lectures. Three
volumes of Dewey's Chinese lectures in English translation, prepared by Dr. Robert Clopton and Dr. Tsuin-chen
Ou, are ready for publication. They are entitled: I,
Social and Political Philosophy; II, Philosophy of Education; and III, Lectures in Philosophy in China.

The appearance of the volume depends on both the de-
signer and the typist. Andor Braun has capably solved
the varied problems of making a work like this one easy
to read and easy to understand. The person responsible
for executing his design is Aldona Johnson, who has
served as much more than the typist--as editor, skilled
craftsman, and perceptive colleague.

Jo Ann Boydston

14 March 1969
Southern Illinois University

Chronological Listing of Translations

Year	Title	Language	Entry Number
1900	*OUTLINES OF A CRITICAL THEORY OF ETHICS*	Jap.	*40a*
	THE SCHOOL AND SOCIETY	Span.	*53dd*
1901	*THE SCHOOL AND SOCIETY*	Jap.	*53n*
1902	*THE PSYCHOLOGY OF NUMBER AND ITS APPLICATION TO METHODS OF TEACHING ARITHMETIC*	Jap.	*48a*
	THE SCHOOL AND SOCIETY [Selection]	Swed.	*53ll*
	"Interest as Related to [the Training of the] Will"	Swed.	*27m*
1904	*THE SCHOOL AND SOCIETY*	Czech	*53e*
1905	*THE SCHOOL AND SOCIETY*	Germ.	*53h*
	THE SCHOOL AND SOCIETY	Jap.	*53o*
1907	*THE SCHOOL AND SOCIETY*	Russ.	*53y*
1909	*THE SCHOOL AND SOCIETY* [Selection]	Fren.	*53hh*
1912	*THE CHILD AND THE CURRICULUM*	Swed.	*4w*
	ETHICS	Jap.	*13a*
	THE SCHOOL AND SOCIETY	Hung.	*53j*
	THE SCHOOL AND SOCIETY [Selection]	Fren.	*53ii*
1913	*THE CHILD AND THE CURRICULUM*	Fren.	*64*
	"The Aim of History in Elementary Education"	Fren.	*64*
	"Ethical Principles Underlying Education"	Fren.	*64*
	"Interest as Related to [the Training of the] Will"	Fren.	*64*
	"My Pedagogic Creed"	Ital.	*36h*
1914	*THE SCHOOL AND SOCIETY* [Selection]	Fren.	*53jj*
1915	*HOW WE THINK*	Russ.	*20l*
	THE SCHOOL AND SOCIETY	Ital.	*53l*

Year	Title	Language	Entry Number
1917	*HOW WE THINK*	Span.	*20n*
	SCHOOLS OF TOMORROW	Swed.	*55m*
	"My Pedagogic Creed"	Span.	*36n*
1918	*DEMOCRACY AND EDUCATION*	Jap.	*8l*
	SCHOOLS OF TOMORROW	Russ.	*55h*
	SCHOOLS OF TOMORROW	Span.	*55k*
1919	*DEMOCRACY AND EDUCATION*	Jap.	*8n*
	GERMAN PHILOSOPHY AND POLITICS [Selection]	Jap.	*18b*
	RECONSTRUCTION IN PHILOSOPHY [Selection]	Jap.	*51u*
1920	*SCHOOLS OF TOMORROW*	Jap.	*55e*
1921	*DEMOCRACY AND EDUCATION* [Selection]	Russ.	*8hh*
	HOW WE THINK	Chin.	*20b*
	MORAL PRINCIPLES IN EDUCATION	Pol.	*35f*
	RECONSTRUCTION IN PHILOSOPHY	Jap.	*51g*
	RECONSTRUCTION IN PHILOSOPHY	Jap.	*51h*
	THE SCHOOL AND SOCIETY	Span.	*53ee*
	"Some Factors in Mutual National Understanding"	Jap.	*57a*
1922	*THE SCHOOL AND SOCIETY*	Russ.	*53aa*
	THE SCHOOL AND THE CHILD	Russ.	*54a*
	SCHOOLS OF TOMORROW [Selection]	Czech	*55q*
	"The Aim of History in Elementary Education"	Bulg.	*1a*
1923	*THE CHILD AND THE CURRICULUM*	Pol.	*64d*
	HUMAN NATURE AND CONDUCT	Jap.	*21f*
	MORAL PRINCIPLES IN EDUCATION	Bulg.	*35b*
	SCHOOLS OF TOMORROW	Chin.	*55c*
	SCHOOLS OF TOMORROW [Selection]	Bulg.	*55o*
	"The Aim of History in Elementary Education"	Pol.	*64d*
	"Ethical Principles Underlying Education"	Pol.	*64d*
	"Interest as Related to [the Training of the] Will"	Pol.	*64d*

Year	Title	Language	Entry Number
1924	*ETHICS*	Jap.	*13b*
	THE SCHOOL AND SOCIETY	Pol.	*53w*
	THE SCHOOL AND SOCIETY	Russ.	*53bb*
	THE SCHOOL AND SOCIETY	Turk.	*53ff*
	SCHOOLS OF TOMORROW	Bulg.	*55b*
1925	*THE CHILD AND THE CURRICULUM*	Bulg.	*4a*
	THE CHILD AND THE CURRICULUM	Span.	*4t*
	EXPERIENCE AND NATURE [Selection]	Czech	*15c*
	HOW WE THINK	Fren.	*20e*
	INTEREST AND EFFORT IN EDUCATION /	Span.	*26h*
	THE SCHOOL AND SOCIETY	Jap.	*53p*
	"My Pedagogic Creed"	Germ.	*36f*
1926	*DEMOCRACY AND EDUCATION* [Selection]	Span.	*65*
	THE SCHOOL AND SOCIETY	Lat.	*53v*
	THE SCHOOL AND THE CHILD	Span.	*54b*
	"Ethical Principles Underlying Education"	Span.	*65*
	"Interest as Related to [the Training of the] Will"	Span.	*65*
	"The Logic of Judgments of Practice"	Czech	*32a*
	"My Pedagogic Creed"	Span.	*65*
	"Psychology and Social Practice"	Span.	*65*
1927	*DEMOCRACY AND EDUCATION* [Selection]	Span.	*8jj*
	DEMOCRACY AND EDUCATION [Selection]	Span.	*8kk*
	"Interest as Related to [the Training of the] Will"	Hung.	*27d*
	"The Rôle of Philosophy in the History of Civilization"	Czech	*52a*
1928	*DEMOCRACY AND EDUCATION*	Turk.	*8y*
	DEMOCRACY AND EDUCATION [Selection]	Arab.	*8z*
	DEMOCRACY AND EDUCATION [Selection]	Span.	*8ll*
	HOW WE THINK	Span.	*20m*
	HOW WE THINK [Selection]	Bulg.	*20p*

Year	Title	Language	Entry Number
1932	*DEMOCRACY AND EDUCATION*	Czech	*8d*
	ETHICS	Urdu	*13e*
1933	*DEMOCRACY AND EDUCATION* [Selection]	Hung.	*8aa*
	HOW WE THINK	Port.	*20j*
	THE SCHOOL AND SOCIETY	Pol.	*53x*
	"Education and Our Present Social Problems"	Span.	*10a*
1934	*THE CHILD AND THE CURRICULUM*	Bulg.	*64a*
	DEMOCRACY AND EDUCATION	Serb.	*8w*
	HOW WE THINK	Pol.	*20i*
	MORAL PRINCIPLES IN EDUCATION	Czech	*35d*
	MORAL PRINCIPLES IN EDUCATION	Turk.	*35g*
	"The Aim of History in Elementary Education"	Bulg.	*64a*
	"Ethical Principles Underlying Education"	Bulg.	*64a*
	"Interest as Related to [the Training of the] Will"	Bulg.	*64a*
1935	*THE CHILD AND THE CURRICULUM*	Germ.	*67*
	HOW WE THINK	Chin.	*20c*
	THE QUEST FOR CERTAINTY	Jap.	*50d*
	THE SCHOOL AND SOCIETY	Bulg.	*53c*
	THE SCHOOL AND SOCIETY	Jap.	*53r*
	THE SCHOOL AND SOCIETY	Serb.	*53cc*
	SCHOOLS OF TOMORROW [Selection]	Bulg.	*55p*
	THE SOURCES OF A SCIENCE OF EDUCATION	Germ.	*67*
	THE WAY OUT OF EDUCATIONAL CONFUSION	Germ.	*67*
	"How Much Freedom in New Schools?"	Germ.	*67*
	"What I Believe"	Bulg.	*63b*
1936	*HOW WE THINK*	Chin.	*20d*
	HUMAN NATURE AND CONDUCT	Swed.	*21l*
	INTEREST AND EFFORT IN EDUCATION	Serb.	*26g*
	THE SOURCES OF A SCIENCE OF EDUCATION	Chin.	*58b*
	"The Need for a Recovery of Philosophy"	Jap.	*37b*
	"The Need for a Recovery of Philosophy"	Jap.	*37c*

Year	Title	Language	Entry Number
1937	*INTEREST AND EFFORT IN EDUCATION*	Bulg.	*26b*
	SCHOOLS OF TOMORROW	Rum.	*55g*
1938	*HUMAN NATURE AND CONDUCT*	Jap.	*21g*
	INTEREST AND EFFORT IN EDUCATION	Hebr.	*26c*
	PHILOSOPHY AND CIVILIZATION	Pol.	*41a*
	SCHOOLS OF TOMORROW	Turk.	*55n*
1939	*EXPERIENCE AND EDUCATION*	Bulg.	*14c*
	EXPERIENCE AND EDUCATION	Span.	*14o*
	THE JOHN DEWEY REPORT	Turk.	*29a*
	RECONSTRUCTION IN PHILOSOPHY	Chin.	*51b*
	SCHOOLS OF TOMORROW	Jap.	*55f*
	"From Absolutism to Experimentalism"	Ital.	*17a*
1940	*THE SCHOOL AND SOCIETY*	Bulg.	*53d*
1941	*EXPERIENCE AND EDUCATION*	Chin.	*14e*
	THE SOURCES OF A SCIENCE OF EDUCATION	Span.	*58h*
	"The Determination of Ultimate Values or Aims through Antecedent or *a priori* Speculation or through Pragmatic or Empirical Inquiry"	Span.	*9a*
	"What I Believe"	Swed.	*63c*
1942	*THE LIVING THOUGHTS OF THOMAS JEFFERSON*	Port.	*31e*
	MESSAGE TO THE CHINESE PEOPLE	Chin.	*34a*
1943	*THE CHILD AND THE CURRICULUM*	Bulg.	*4c*
1944	*ETHICS* [Selection: *THEORY OF THE MORAL LIFE*]	Span.	*13j*
	THE LIVING THOUGHTS OF THOMAS JEFFERSON	Span.	*31f*
1945	*EXPERIENCE AND EDUCATION*	Arab.	*14a*
1946	*DEMOCRACY AND EDUCATION*	Bulg.	*8b*
	DEMOCRACY AND EDUCATION	Span.	*8x*
	EXPERIENCE AND EDUCATION	Chin.	*14f*
	FREEDOM AND CULTURE	Span.	*16o*
	LIBERALISM AND SOCIAL ACTION	Ital.	*30a*

Year	Title	Language	Entry Number
1947	*THE CHILD AND THE CURRICULUM*	Chin.	*4e*
	THE CHILD AND THE CURRICULUM	Kor.	*64c*
	EXPERIENCE AND EDUCATION	Fren.	*14h*
	EXPERIENCE AND EDUCATION	Kor.	*14n*
	PROBLEMS OF MEN [Selection]	Russ.	*44d*
	THE SCHOOL AND SOCIETY	Kor.	*53u*
	THE SOURCES OF A SCIENCE OF EDUCATION	Czech	*58c*
	"The Aim of History in Elementary Education"	Kor.	*64c*
	"Ethical Principles Underlying Education"	Kor.	*64c*
	"Interest as Related to [the Training of the] Will"	Kor.	*64c*
1948	*DEMOCRACY AND EDUCATION* [Selection]	Kor.	*8dd*
	DEMOCRACY AND EDUCATION [Selection]	Swed.	*8mm*
	EXPERIENCE AND EDUCATION	Chin.	*14g*
	EXPERIENCE AND NATURE	Span.	*15b*
	EXPERIENCE AND NATURE [Selection]	Ital.	*15d*
	INDIVIDUALISM, OLD AND NEW	Ital.	*23b*
	THE SCHOOL AND SOCIETY	Iran.	*53k*
1949	*ART AS EXPERIENCE*	Span.	*3d*
	DEMOCRACY AND EDUCATION	Ital.	*8j*
	EDUCATION TODAY	Arab.	*11a*
	LOGIC: THE THEORY OF INQUIRY	Ital.	*33c*
	RECONSTRUCTION IN PHILOSOPHY [Selection]	Germ.	*51q*
	THE SCHOOL AND SOCIETY	Ital.	*53m*
	"From Absolutism to Experimentalism"	Span.	*17b*
1950	*THE CHILD AND THE CURRICULUM*	Ital.	*64b*
	EDUCATION TODAY	Ital.	*11b*
	EXPERIENCE AND EDUCATION	Ital.	*14l*
	EXPERIENCE AND EDUCATION	Jap.	*14m*
	HOW WE THINK	Jap.	*20h*
	INDIVIDUALISM, OLD AND NEW [Selection]	Ital.	*23d*
	LOGIC: THE THEORY OF INQUIRY	Span.	*33e*
	PROBLEMS OF MEN	Ital.	*44b*
	RECONSTRUCTION IN PHILOSOPHY	Jap.	*51i*

Year	Title	Language	Entry Number
1950 (Cont.)	*THE SCHOOL AND SOCIETY*	Jap.	*53s*
	"The Aim of History in Elementary Education"	Ital.	*64b*
	"Ethical Principles Underlying Education"	Ital.	*64b*
	"Interest as Related to [the Training of the] Will"	Ital.	*64b*
	"My Pedagogic Creed"	Jap.	*36k*
	"My Pedagogic Creed"	Span.	*36r*
	"The Objectivism-Subjectivism of Modern Philosophy"	Ital.	*39a*
1951	*ART AS EXPERIENCE*	Ital.	*3b*
	A COMMON FAITH	Jap.	*5b*
	EDUCATION TODAY	Span.	*11c*
	FREEDOM AND CULTURE	Jap.	*16i*
	HOW WE THINK	Germ.	*20f*
	HUMAN NATURE AND CONDUCT	Jap.	*21h*
	RECONSTRUCTION IN PHILOSOPHY [Selection]	Ital.	*51r*
	THE SOURCES OF A SCIENCE OF EDUCATION	Ital.	*58f*
	"The Social-Economic Situation and Education"	Span.	*56a*
1952	*ART AS EXPERIENCE*	Jap.	*3c*
	THE JOHN DEWEY REPORT	Turk.	*29b*
	THE LIVING THOUGHTS OF THOMAS JEFFERSON	Ital.	*31d*
	PROBLEMS OF MEN	Span.	*44c*
	THE QUEST FOR CERTAINTY	Span.	*50f*
1953	*FREEDOM AND CULTURE*	Chin.	*16b*
	FREEDOM AND CULTURE	Ital.	*16h*
	FREEDOM AND CULTURE	Port.	*16n*
1954	*DEMOCRACY AND EDUCATION*	Arab.	*8a*
	DEMOCRACY AND EDUCATION [Selection]	Ital.	*66*
	EDUCATION TODAY [Selections]	Ital.	*66*
	EXPERIENCE AND EDUCATION	Arab.	*14b*
	EXPERIENCE AND EDUCATION	Greek	*14j*
	EXPERIENCE AND EDUCATION [Selection]	Ital.	*66*
	FREEDOM AND CULTURE	Chin.	*16c*
	FREEDOM AND CULTURE	Kor.	*16k*
	GERMAN PHILOSOPHY AND POLITICS	Germ.	*18a*

Year	Title	Language	Entry Number
1954 (Cont.)	*THE SCHOOL AND SOCIETY* [Selection]	Ital.	*66*
	"My Pedagogic Creed"	Ital.	*66*
1955	*DEMOCRACY AND EDUCATION*	Kor.	*8r*
	FREEDOM AND CULTURE	Arab.	*16a*
	FREEDOM AND CULTURE	Fren.	*16d*
	FREEDOM AND CULTURE	Greek	*16f*
	RECONSTRUCTION IN PHILOSOPHY	Mala.	*51k*
	RECONSTRUCTION IN PHILOSOPHY	Span.	*51o*
1956	*FREEDOM AND CULTURE*	Germ.	*16e*
	HUMAN NATURE AND CONDUCT	Iran.	*21d*
	HUMAN NATURE AND CONDUCT	Port.	*21j*
	"The Pragmatism of Peirce"	Ital.	*43a*
1957	*FREEDOM AND CULTURE*	Kann.	*16j*
	HOW WE THINK [Selection?]	Turk.	*20o*
	JOHN DEWEY: HIS CONTRIBUTION TO THE AMERICAN TRADITION	Kor.	*28b*
	THE LIVING THOUGHTS OF THOMAS JEFFERSON	Arab.	*31a*
	PROBLEMS OF MEN	Hindi	*44a*
	THE QUEST FOR CERTAINTY	Greek	*50b*
	RECONSTRUCTION IN PHILOSOPHY	Arab.	*51a*
	RECONSTRUCTION IN PHILOSOPHY	Tamil	*51p*
	THE SCHOOL AND SOCIETY	Finn.	*53g*
	THEORY OF VALUATION	Jap.	*60b*
	"The Need for a Recovery of Philosophy"	Ital.	*37a*
1958	*FREEDOM AND CULTURE*	Mara.	*16m*
	FREEDOM AND CULTURE	Tamil	*16q*
	HUMAN NATURE AND CONDUCT	Ital.	*21e*
	THE PUBLIC AND ITS PROBLEMS	Span.	*49a*
	RECONSTRUCTION IN PHILOSOPHY	Iran.	*51e*
	RECONSTRUCTION IN PHILOSOPHY	Port.	*51l*
	THEORY OF VALUATION	Span.	*60c*
	"Unity of Science as a Social Problem"	Ital.	*61a*
1959	*A COMMON FAITH*	Ital.	*5a*
	DEMOCRACY AND EDUCATION	Kor.	*8s*
	DEMOCRACY AND EDUCATION	Mara.	*8t*
	EXPERIENCE AND NATURE	Jap.	*15a*
	FREEDOM AND CULTURE	Mala.	*16l*
	HOW WE THINK	Port.	*20k*

Year	Title	Language	Entry Number
1959	*RECONSTRUCTION IN PHILOSOPHY*	Port.	*51m*
(Cont.)	"My Pedagogic Creed"	Arab.	*36a*
	"My Pedagogic Creed"	Chin.	*36b*
	"My Pedagogic Creed"	Jap.	*36l*
	"My Pedagogic Creed"	Span.	*36u*
	"What I Believe"	Arab.	*63a*
1960	*THE CHILD AND THE CURRICULUM*	Hebr.	*4h*
	A COMMON FAITH	Jap.	*5c*
	DEMOCRACY AND EDUCATION	Hebr.	*8h*
	ETHICS [Selection: *THEORY OF THE MORAL LIFE*]	Jap.	*13g*
	EXPERIENCE AND EDUCATION	Hebr.	*14k*
	INDIVIDUALISM, OLD AND NEW	Arab.	*23a*
	INDIVIDUALISM, OLD AND NEW	Jap.	*23c*
	JOHN DEWEY: HIS CONTRIBUTION TO THE AMERICAN TRADITION	Port.	*28c*
	LIBERALISM AND SOCIAL ACTION	Jap.	*30b*
	LOGIC: THE THEORY OF INQUIRY	Arab.	*33a*
	THE QUEST FOR CERTAINTY	Arab.	*50a*
	RECONSTRUCTION IN PHILOSOPHY	Kor.	*51j*
	THE SCHOOL AND SOCIETY	Hebr.	*53i*
	THE SOURCES OF A SCIENCE OF EDUCATION	Hebr.	*58e*
	THEORY OF VALUATION	Ital.	*60a*
1961	*DEMOCRACY AND EDUCATION*	Iran.	*8i*
	HOW WE THINK	Ital.	*20g*
	JOHN DEWEY: HIS CONTRIBUTION TO THE AMERICAN TRADITION	Jap.	*28a*
	THE LIVING THOUGHTS OF THOMAS JEFFERSON	Arab.	*31b*
	MORAL PRINCIPLES IN EDUCATION	Jap.	*35e*
	"Some Aspects of Modern Education" [Same as *AMERICAN EDUCATION PAST AND FUTURE*]	Span.	*2b*
1962	*ETHICS*	Jap.	*13d*
	FREEDOM AND CULTURE	Turk.	*16r*
	LOGIC: THE THEORY OF INQUIRY	Serb.	*33d*
	"Conduct and Experience"	Span.	*6a*
1963	*ART AS EXPERIENCE*	Arab.	*3a*
	DEMOCRACY AND EDUCATION	Pol.	*8u*

Year	Title	Language	Entry Number
1963 (Cont.)	*ETHICS* [Selection: *THEORY OF THE MORAL LIFE*]	Hindi	*13f*
	EXPERIENCE AND EDUCATION	Germ.	*14i*
	HUMAN NATURE AND CONDUCT	Arab.	*21a*
	HUMAN NATURE AND CONDUCT	Hindi	*21c*
	HUMAN NATURE AND CONDUCT	Kor.	*21i*
	THE LIVING THOUGHTS OF THOMAS JEFFERSON	Indo.	*31c*
1964	*A COMMON FAITH*	Span.	*5d*
	DEMOCRACY AND EDUCATION	Guja.	*8g*
	ETHICS [Selection: *THEORY OF THE MORAL LIFE*]	Port.	*13h*
	ETHICS [Selection: *THEORY OF THE MORAL LIFE*]	Urdu	*13k*
	HUMAN NATURE AND CONDUCT	Span.	*21k*
	THE SCHOOL AND SOCIETY	Arab.	*53b*
	"My Pedagogic Creed"	Hebr.	*36g*
1965	*DEMOCRACY AND EDUCATION*	Ital.	*8k*
	FREEDOM AND CULTURE	Hindi	*16g*
	FREEDOM AND CULTURE	Span.	*16p*
	RECONSTRUCTION IN PHILOSOPHY	Chin.	*51c*
	SCHOOLS OF TOMORROW	Arab.	*55a*
	"Spencer and Bergson"	Fren.	*59a*
1966	*ETHICS* [Selection: *THEORY OF THE MORAL LIFE*]	Punj.	*13i*
	INTELLIGENCE IN THE MODERN WORLD	Chin.	*25a*
	LOGIC: THE THEORY OF INQUIRY	Fren.	*33b*
	MORAL PRINCIPLES IN EDUCATION	Arab.	*35a*
	THE QUEST FOR CERTAINTY	Ital.	*50c*
	THE SOURCES OF A SCIENCE OF EDUCATION	Jap.	*58g*
Date Doubtful	*MORAL PRINCIPLES IN EDUCATION*	Chin.	*35c*
	THE SOURCES OF A SCIENCE OF EDUCATION	Chin.	*58a*
	"My Pedagogic Creed"	Chin.	*36c*

CONTENTS

Language Abbreviations

Arabic	Arab.
Armenian	Arm.
Bulgarian	Bulg.
Chinese	Chin.
Czech	Czech
Dutch	Dutch
English	Eng.
Finnish	Finn.
French	Fren.
German	Germ.
Greek	Greek
Gujarati	Guja.
Hebrew	Hebr.
Hindi	Hindi
Hungarian	Hung.
Indonesian	Indo.
Iranian	Iran.
Italian	Ital.
Japanese	Jap.
Kannada	Kann.
Korean	Kor.
Latvian	Lat.
Malayalam	Mala.
Marathi	Mara.
Polish	Pol.
Portuguese	Port.
Punjabi	Punj.
Rumanian	Rum.
Russian	Russ.
Serbo-Croatian	Serb.
Spanish	Span.
Swedish	Swed.
Tamil	Tamil
Turkish	Turk.
Urdu	Urdu

I Books, Articles, Pamphlets, Monographs, and Collections

1. "The Aim of History in Elementary Education,"
   The Elementary School Record, No. 8 (Nov. 1900),
   199-203.

   a. [Bulg.] "Celta na obučenieto po istorijata v
      osnovnoto učilište." Trans. "B." In
      Svobodno văzpitanie, I, 6 (1922-23),
      185-89.

   b. [Bulg.] "Celta na obučenieto po istorijata v
      osnovnoto učilište," in *Učilisteto i
      deteto*, [pp.?]. [*See 64a*]

   c. [Fren.] "Le but de l'histoire dans l'instruc-
      tion primaire," in *L'école et l'enfant*,
      pp. 119-28. [*See 64*]

   d. [Ital.] "L'insegnamento della storia," in
      Saggi pedagogici, [pp.?]. [*See 64b*]

   e. [Kor.] [Title?] In *Hakkyo wa adong*, [pp.?].
      [*See 64c*]

   f. [Pol.] [Title?] In *Szkola i dziecko*, [pp.?].
      [*See 64d*]

   g. [Pol.] [Title?] In *Szkola i dziecko*, [pp.?].
      [*See 64e*]

   h. [Rum.] [Title?] In *Şcoala şi copilul*, [pp.?].
      [*See 64f*]

   i. [Rum.] [Title?] In *Şcoala şi copilul*, [pp.?].
      [*See 64g*]

   j. [Russ.] [Title?] In *Shkola i rebënok*, [pp.?].
      [*See 54a*]

   k. [Span.] "La finalidad de la historia en la
      escuela primaria," in *La escuela y el
      niño*, [pp.?]. [*See 54b*]

   l. [Span.] "La finalidad de la historia en la
      escuela primaria." [Trans.?] In
      Magisterio, 24 (May 1929), [pp.?].

2. AMERICAN EDUCATION PAST AND FUTURE
   Chicago: University of Chicago Press, [c1931].

14 pp. [Printed with the title "Some Aspects of Modern Education," in *School and Society*, XXXIV (31 Oct. 1931), 579-84.]

a. [Span.] [Title?] [Trans.?] In *Revista de pedagogía*, X (1931), 554-60.

b. [Span.] "Algunos aspectos de la educación moderna." [Trans.?] In *Ideas pedagógicas del siglo XX*, ed. Lorenzo Luzuriaga, pp. 11-19. Buenos Aires: Losada, 1961.

3. ART AS EXPERIENCE
   New York: Minton, Balch and Co., [c1934].
   vii, 355 pp.
   [London: G. Allen and Unwin, 1934. 355 pp.]
   [New York: Capricorn Books, G. P. Putnam's Sons, 1959. 355 pp.]

a. [Arab.] *al-Fann Khibrah*. Trans. Zakarīyā Ibrāhīm [rev. by Zakī Najīb Maḥmūd]. Cairo: Dār al-Nahḍah al-'Arabīyah, 1963. 599 pp.

b. [Ital.] *L'arte come esperienza*. Trans. [with an introd. by] Corrado Maltese. (Pensatori del Nostro Tempo, II) Florence: La Nuova Italia, 1951. 411 pp.
   2nd printing, 1960. xxxii, 416 pp.
   3rd printing, 1966
   4th printing, 1967

c. [Jap.] *Keiken to shite no geijutsu*. Trans. Yashushi Suzuki. Tokyo: Shunjūsha, 1952. 424 pp.

d. [Span.] *El arte como experiencia*. Trans. [with an introd. by] Samuel Ramos. (Obras de Filosofía) México, D.F., Buenos Aires: Fondo de Cultura Económica, 1949. xxi, 315 pp.
   2nd printing, 1950

4. THE CHILD AND THE CURRICULUM
   (University of Chicago Contributions to Educa-
   tion, No. V) Chicago: University of
   Chicago Press, 1902. 40 pp.

a. [Bulg.] "Deteto i učebnite programi." [Trans.?]
   In *Učilišten pregled*, XXIV, 1-2 (1925),
   56-70.

b. [Bulg.] "Deteto i učebnite programi," in
   Učilišteto i deteto, [pp.?] [*See 64a*]

c. [Bulg.] "Deteto i učebnata materija." Trans.
   Ivan Skačokov. In *Svobodno vǎzpitanie*,
   XXII, 5-10 (1943-44), 97-116.

d. [Bulg.] *Deteto i učebnata materija*. Trans.
   Ivan Skačokov. Sofia: St. Georgiev,
   1944. 22 pp.

e. [Chin.] *Ehr-t'ung yü chiao-ts'ai*. Trans.
   Tsung-hai Cheng. Shanghai: Chung Hua
   Book Co., 1947. iv, 28 pp.

f. [Fren.] "L'enfant et les programmes d'études,"
   in *L'école et l'enfant*, pp. 91-118.
   [*See 64*]

g. [Germ.] "Das Kind und der Lehrplan," in *Der
   Projekt-Plan*, pp. 142-60. [*See 67*]

h. [Hebr.] *Ha-yeled ve-tokhnit ha-limudim*. Trans.
   Haim Braver [with an introd. by P. A.
   Kleinberger], [pp.?]. Tel-Aviv: Otzar
   Hamoreh, 1960. [Includes *53i*]

i. [Hung.] "A gondolkodás nevelése: A gyermek és
   a tanterv." Trans. Elemér Kenyeres.
   In *Kisdednevelés*, 6 (1930), 167-81.

j. [Hung.] *A gondolkodás nevelése: A gyermek és
   a tanterv*. Trans. Elemér Kenyeres.
   Budapest: Kisdednevelés, 1931. 60 pp.

k. [Ital.] "Il fanciullo e i problemi scolastici,"
   in *Saggi pedagogici*, [pp.?]. [*See 64b*]

l. [Kor.] [Title?] In *Hakkyo wa adong*, [pp.?].
   [*See 64c*]

m. [Pol.]   [Title?] In *Szkoła i dziecko*, [pp.?].
             [*See 64d*]

n. [Pol.]   [Title?] In *Szkoła i dziecko*, [pp.?].
             [*See 64e*]

o. [Port.]   "A criança e o programa escolar."
             Trans. [with an introd. by] Anísio S.
             Teixeira [ed. Lourenço Filho]. In
             Vida e educação, Pt. I, [pp.?]. (Bib-
             lioteca de Educação, XII) São Paulo:
             Companhia Melhoramentos de São Paulo,
             [n.d., Pref. 1930]. [Includes *26e*]
                        2nd printing, [n.d., Pref.
                          1930]
                        3rd printing, 1952
                        4th printing, [n.d.]
                        5th printing, [1954?]
                        6th printing, [1958?]

p. [Port.]   "A criança e o programa escolar."
             Trans. [with an introd. by] Anísio S.
             Teixeira [ed. Lourenço Filho]. In
             Vida e educação, Pt. I, [pp.?]. (Bib-
             lioteca Pedagógica Brasileira, Atuali-
             dades Pedagógicas, LXXVI) São Paulo:
             Companhia Editôra Nacional, 1959.
             [Includes *26f*]
                        2nd printing, 1962

q. [Rum.]   [Title?] In *Şcoala şi copilul*, [pp.?].
             [*See 64f*]

r. [Rum.]   [Title?] In *Şcoala şi copilul*, [pp.?].
             [*See 64g*]

s. [Russ.]   [Title?] In *Shkola i rebĕnok*, [pp.?].
             [*See 54a*]

t. [Span.]   *El niño y el programa escolar*. Trans.
             [with an introd. by] Lorenzo Luzuriaga.
             (Publicaciones de la Revista de Pedago-
             gía, La Pedagogía Contemporánea, I)
             Madrid: Revista de Pedagogía, 1925.
             48 pp.
                        2nd printing, 1930
                        3rd printing, 1934

u. [Span.]   "El niño y el programa escolar," in
             La escuela y el niño, [pp.?]. [*See 54b*]

v. [Span.] *El niño y el programa escolar. Mi
credo pedagógico.* Trans. [with an
introd. by] Lorenzo Luzuriaga. Buenos
Aires: Losada, 1959. 137 pp. [In-
cludes *36u*]
        2nd printing, 1963. 142 pp.

w. [Swed.] "Barnet och skolkursen." Trans. Agnes
Undén Jacobsson. In *Pragmatiska
uppfostringsprinciper jämte Barnet och
skolkursen av John Dewey*, by Malte
Jacobsson, pp. 75-170. Lund: C. W. K.
Gleerups Förlag, 1912.

The Child and the Curriculum [Selection(s)].

x. [Span.] "Conocimientos y personalidad."
[Selection from *4s*] In *Boletín de la
I.M.A.*, No. 6 (May 1929), 15.

y. [Swed.] "Barnet och skolkursen," [extract].
Trans. Agnes Undén Jacobsson. In
*Källor till uppfostrans och de peda-
gogiska reformidéernas historia*, by
B. R. Hall, pp. 151-56. Stockholm:
P. A. Norstedt and Sons, 1913.

z. [Swed.] "Barnet och skolkursen," [extract].
Trans. Agnes Undén Jacobsson. In
Andra bearbetade upplagen, by B. R.
Hall, pp. 105-8. Stockholm: P. A.
Norstedt and Sons, 1920.

5. A COMMON FAITH
   New Haven: Yale University Press; London:
      Humphrey Milford, Oxford University
      Press, 1934. 87 pp.

a. [Ital.] *Una fede comune.* Trans. [with an
introd. by] Guido Calogero. Florence:
La Nuova Italia, 1959. xxxii, 96 pp.
        2nd printing, 1961
        3rd printing, 1966
        4th printing, 1967

b. [Jap.] *Dardemo no shinkō.* Trans. Hideo
Kishimoto. Tokyo: Shunjūsha, 1951.
135 pp.

c. [Jap.] "Shikyōron." Trans. Kazuo Nakabashi and Yūjirō Nakamura. In *Dyūi*, pp. 199-248. (Sekai Dai Shisō Zenshū, XIX) Tokyo: Kawade Shobō, 1960.

d. [Span.] *Una fe común.* Trans. Josefina Martínez Alinari. Buenos Aires: Losada, 1964. 98 pp.

A Common Faith [Selection(s)].

e. [Jap.] "Kyōtsū keiken no shukyo" ("The Religion of Shared Experience"). In *Jyon Dyūi; sono tetsugaku no gendai eno kiyo*, pp. 343-55. [*See 28a*]

f. [Kor.] "Konggwandoen kyŏnghŏm ŭi chonggyo," in *Dyui sŏnjip*, pp. 333-46. [*See 28b*]

g. [Port.] [Title?] In *John Dewey, sua contribuição para a tradição americana*, [pp.?]. [*See 28c*]

6. "Conduct and Experience," in *Psychologies of 1930*, pp. 409-22. Ed. Carl Murchison. Worcester, Mass.: Clark University Press, 1930.

a. [Span.] "Herencia, conducta y motivación." Trans. Elizabeth Jelin and J. J. Thomas. In [Title?] (*Psychologies of 1930*), [pp.?]. Buenos Aires: Paidós, 1962.

7. "Creative Democracy--The Task Before Us," in *The Philosopher of the Common Man*, pp. 220-28. New York: G. P. Putnam's Sons, 1940.

a. [Jap.] "Dotokuteki riso to shite no minshushugi" ("Democracy as a Moral Ideal"). In *Jyon Dyūi; sono tetsugaku no gendai eno kiyo*, pp. 356-65. [*See 28a*]

b. [Kor.] "Todŏkchŏk isang ŭrosŏŭi minjujuŭi," in *Dyui sŏnjip*, pp. 347-56. [*See 28b*]

c. [Port.] [Title?] In *John Dewey, sua contribuição para a tradição americana,* [pp.?].
[*See 28c*]

8. DEMOCRACY AND EDUCATION: An Introduction to the
Philosophy of Education
New York: The Macmillan Co., 1916.
xii, 434 pp.

al-Dīmuqrātīyah wa-al-tarbiyah. Trans.
Mattā 'Aqrāwī and Zakarīyā Mīkhā'īl.
Cairo: Maṭba'at Lajnat al-Ta'līf wa-
al-Tarjamah, [n.d.]. 376 pp.
2nd printing, 1954

b. [Bulg.] *Demokracija i obrazovanie: V̆avedenie
v̆av filosofijata na obrazovanieto.*
Trans. Hrizantema Ognjanova Čohadžieva
[ed. G. D. Pir'ov]. Sofia: National
Ministry of Culture and Information,
1946. 412 pp.

c. [Chin.] *Min-pen chu-i yü chiao-yü.* Trans.
Chou En-jun. Shanghai: The Commercial Press, 1929. 5 vols. 653 pp.
[Taipei (Taiwan) ed., 1960. 2 vols.
653 pp.]

d. [Czech] *Demokracie a výchova.* Trans. Josef
Hrůša. Prague: J. Laichter, 1932.
503 pp.

e. [Germ.] *Demokratie und Erziehung: Eine
Einleitung in die philosophische
Pädagogik.* Trans. [with a foreword by]
Erich Hylla. Breslau: Ferdinand Hirt,
1930. 565 pp.

f. [Germ.] *Demokratie und Erziehung: Eine
Einleitung in die philosophische
Pädagogik.* Trans. [with a foreword by]
Erich Hylla. Braunschweig, Berlin,
Hamburg: Georg Westermann Verlag,
1949. 488 pp.
2nd printing, 1964

g. [Guja.] *Sikshan ane loksahi.* Trans. Amrital
Bhagvanji Yajnik. Bombay: Vora, 1964.
x, 656 pp.

h. [Hebr.] *Demokratyah ve-hinukh: Mavo le-*
philosophya shel-ha-hinukh. Trans.
[with a foreword by] Yomtov Helman.
(Sifray Mofet Me-sifrut Ha-olam)
Jerusalem: Bialik Institute, 1960.
xxvii, 302 pp.

i. [Iran.] *Democraci va Āmūzesh va Parvaresh.*
Trans. E. Ārīyānpūr. Tehran [Tabriz?]:
Franklin, 1961. 240 pp.
2nd printing, 1962

j. [Ital.] *Democrazia ed educazione.* Trans. Enzo
Enriques Agnoletti. (Educatori Antichi
e Moderni, LX) Florence: La Nuova
Italia, 1949. xii, 488 pp.
2nd printing, Feb. 1951.
xii, 484 pp.
3rd printing, Dec. 1951
4th printing, 1953
5th printing, 1954
6th printing, 1959
7th printing, 1961
8th printing, 1963

k. [Ital.] *Democrazia ed educazione.* Trans. Enzo
Enriques Agnoletti; re-trans. [in part
by] Paolo Paduano. Florence: La Nuova
Italia, 1965. xii, 462 pp.
2nd printing, 1967

l. [Jap.] *Mimponshugi no kyōiku.* Trans. Sajū
Tasei. Tokyo: Ryūbunkan, 1918. 410
pp.

m. [Jap.] *Mimponshugi no kyōiku.* Trans. Sajū
Tasei. (Sekai Dai Shisō Zenshū)
Tokyo: Shunjūsha, 1927. 150 pp.

n. [Jap.] *Kyōiku tetsugaku gairon (Introduction*
to the Philosophy of Education). Trans.
Riichirō Hoashi. Tokyo: Rakuyōdō,
1919. 603 pp. ["According to the
translator, the word 'democracy,' if
used in print at this time, would have
created problems with the governmental
authorities."--Victor N. Kobayashi.]

o. [Jap.] *Kyōiku tetsugaku gairon (Introduction*

to the *Philosophy of Education*). Trans.
Riichirō Hoashi. Tokyo: Shinseidō,
1924. 592 pp.
    2nd printing, 1929

p. [Jap.] *Mimponshugi to kyōiku*. Trans. Riichirō
Hoashi. Tokyo: Shunjūsha, 1948. 423
pp. [Pref. by Dewey in English.]
    2nd printing, 1950
    3rd printing, 1952
    4th printing, 1954
    5th printing, 1959

q. [Jap.] *Minshushugi to kyōiku*. Trans. Riichirō
Hoashi. Tokyo: Tamagawa Daigaku
Shuppanbu, 1955. v, 455 pp.
    2nd printing, 1959

r. [Kor.] *Minjujuǔi wa kyoyuk*. Trans. Han-yǒng
Yim and Ch'ǒn-sǒk O. Seoul: Haptong
Tosǒ Chusik Hoesa, 1955. 648 pp.

s. [Kor.] *Minjujuǔi wa kyoyuk*. Trans. Ch'ǒn-sǒk
O. Seoul: Han'guk Pǒnyǒk Tosǒ Chusik
Hoesa, 1959. 648 pp.

t. [Mara.] *Lokashahi ani shikshan: Shaikshanik
tattvadnyanacha parichay*. Trans.
Ganesh Vinayak Akolkar. Poona: A. V.
Gruha Prakashan, 1959. 410 pp.
    2nd printing, [1961?]

u. [Pol.] *Democracja i wychowanie: Wstęp do
filozofii wychowania*. Trans. Zofja
Bastgenówna [with an introd. by B.
Suchodolski]. Warsaw: Książka i
Wiedza, 1963. 1i, 413 pp.

v. [Port.] *Democracia e educação: Breve tratado
de filosofia de educação*. Trans.
Godofredo Rangel and Anísio S. Teixeira.
(Biblioteca Pedagógica Brasileira,
Atualidades Pedagógicas, XXI) São
Paulo: Companhia Editôra Nacional,
[1930?]. [pp.?]
    2nd printing, 1936. 439 pp.
    3rd printing, 1952. 470 pp.
    4th printing, 1959. 416 pp.
    [Subtitle: *Introdução à*

filosofia da educação.]
5th printing, 1962

w. [Serb.] *Demokracia i obrazovanie.* Trans.
Dragomir Ikonić. Belgrade: A. D.
Geca Kon, 1934. vi, 597 pp.

x. [Span.] *Democracia y educación: Una introduc-*
ción a la filosofía de la educación.
Trans. Lorenzo Luzuriaga. Buenos Aires:
Losada, 1946. 397 pp.
2nd printing, 1953. 374 pp.
3rd printing, 1957. 358 pp.
4th printing, 1960. 361 pp.
5th printing, 1963. 358 pp.
6th printing, 1964. 382 pp.

y. [Turk.] *Demokrasi ve terbiye.* Trans. Başman
Avni [with an introd. by Mehmed Emin].
Istanbul: Türkiye Cumhuriyeti Maarif
Vekâleti, 1928. 426 pp.

Democracy and Education [Selection(s)].

z. [Arab.] *Risālah fī falsafat al-Tarbiyah al-*
Hadīthah (A Message in the Philosophy
of Education). Trans. Ihsān Ahmad al-
Qūsī. Cairo: Matba'at al-Ma'ārif,
1928. 69 pp.

aa. [Hung.] *John Dewey; neveléstana (John Dewey:*
Educator). [*Demokrácia és nevelés.*]
Trans. Samu Szemere. Budapest: Kis-
dednevelés, 1933. 88 pp.

bb. [Ital.] *Democrazia ed educazione,* Chs. X, XI,
and XII. [*See 8j*] In *Il mio credo*
pedagogico, pp. 105-76. [*See 66*]

cc. [Jap.] "Kyōiku no tetsugaku" ("Philosophy as
Education"). In *John Dyūi; sono tetsu-*
gaku no gendai eno kiyo, pp. 88-237.
[*See 28a*]

dd. [Kor.] *Minjujuŭi wa kyoyuk.* Trans. Ch'ŏn-sŏk
O. Seoul: Kukche Munhwasa, 1948.
243 pp.

ee. [Kor.] "Kyoyuk ch'ŏrhak," in *Dyui sŏnjip,*
pp. 95-230. [*See 28b*]

ff. [Port.] "A educação como necessidade da vida"
("Education as a Necessity of Life").
Trans. Godofredo Rangel and Anísio S.
Teixeira. In *Atualidades pedagógicas*,
X, 48 (Sept.-Dec. 1959), 17-20.

gg. [Port.] "A filosofia como educação" ("Philosophy as Education"). In *John Dewey, sua
contribuição para a tradição americana*,
pp. 90-220. [*See 28c*]

hh. [Russ.] *Vvednie v filosofiyu vospitaniya.*
Trans. [with an introd. by] S. T.
Shatskii. Moscow: [n.p.], 1921.
62 pp.

ii. [Span.] "El interés y la disciplina," in
Ensayos de educación, pp. 100-128.
[*See 65*]

jj. [Span.] *Teorías sobre la educación.* [Trans.?]
(Ciencia y Educación, Sección Contem-
poránea, Obras de Dewey, III) Madrid:
La Lectura, 1927. 213 pp.
[Contents: "La educación como una
necesidad de la vida," pp. 13-29.
"La educación como una función social,"
pp. 31-56.
"La educación como dirección," pp.
57-91.
"La educación como un crecimiento,"
pp. 93-118.
"Preparación, desarrollo y disciplina
formal," pp. 119-49.
"La educación como conservadora y
como progresiva," pp. 151-73.
"La concepción democrática en la
educación," pp. 175-213.]

kk. [Span.] *Los fines, las materias y los métodos
de la educación.* [Trans.?] (Ciencia
y Educación, Sección Contemporánea,
Obras de Dewey, IV) Madrid: La
Lectura, 1927. 279 pp.
[Contents: "Los fines de la educación,"
pp. 7-29.
"El desenvolvimiento natural y la
eficacia social como aspiración,"
pp. 31-57.

"El interés y la disciplina," pp. 59-87.
"La experiencia y el pensamiento," pp.
    89-115.
"El pensamiento en la educación," pp.
    117-41.
"La naturaleza del método," pp. 143-75.
"La naturaleza de la materia de estu-
    dio," pp. 177-204.
"El juego y las ocupaciones activas en
    el programa," pp. 205-30.
"La significación de la geografía y de
    la historia," pp. 231-54.
"La ciencia en el programa de estudios,"
    255-79.]

11. [Span.]   *Filosofía de la educación. Los valores
              educativos.* [Trans.?] (Ciencia y Edu-
              cación, Sección Contemporánea, Obras de
              Dewey, V) Madrid: La Lectura, 1928.
              271 pp.
              [Contents: "Los valores educativos,"
                  pp. 7-44.
              "Trabajo y ocio," pp. 45-68.
              "Estudios intelectuales y prácticos,"
                  pp. 69-99.
              "Estudios físicos y sociales. Natura-
                  lismo y humanismo," pp. 101-28.
              "El individuo y el mundo," pp. 129-59.
              "El aspecto vocacional de la educación,"
                  pp. 161-90.
              "Filosofía de la educación," pp. 191-213.
              "Teorías del conocimiento," pp. 215-39.
              "Teorías de la moral," pp. 241-70.]

mm. [Swed.]   *Demokrati och uppfostran.* Trans. [with
              a foreword by] Alf Ahlberg. Stockholm:
              Natur och Kultur, 1948. 152 pp.

9.   "The Determination of Ultimate Values or Aims
     through Antecedent or *a priori* Speculation or
                 through Pragmatic or Empirical Inquiry,"
                 in *Thirty-seventh Yearbook* of the Na-
                 tional Society for the Study of Educa-
                 tion, Pt. II, pp. 471-85. Bloomington:
                 Ill.: Public School Publishing Co., 1938.

a. [Span.]   "La filosofía de la educación," in

La ciencia de la educación, Pt. II, pp.
81-103. [*See 58h*]

10. "Education and Our Present Social Problems,"
School and Society, XXXVII (15 Apr. 1933),
473-78; *Educational Method*, XII (Apr.
1933), 385-90.

  a. [Span.] "La educación y los problemas sociales
actuales." Trans. Lorenzo Luzuriaga.
In *Revista de pedagogía* (Madrid), XII,
140 (Aug. 1933), 337-44.

11. EDUCATION TODAY
Ed. [with a foreword by] Joseph Ratner. New
York: G. P. Putnam's Sons [c1940].
xix, 376 pp.

  a. [Arab.] [Title?] Trans. Abdul Aziz Majid, *et
al*. Cairo: [n.p.], 1949. [pp.?]

  b. [Ital.] *L'educazione di oggi*. Trans. Lamberto
Borghi. (Educatori Antichi e Moderni,
LXXII) Florence: La Nuova Italia,
1950. xx, 470 pp.
                2nd printing, 1953
                3rd printing, 1961

  c. [Span.] *La educación de hoy*. Trans. Carlos
Luzuriaga. (Biblioteca Pedagógica)
Buenos Aires: Losada, 1951. 193 pp.
                2nd printing, 1957
                3rd printing, 1960. 195 pp.
                4th printing, 1965. 199 pp.

    Education Today [Selection(s)].

  d. [Ital.] "Democrazia ed administrazione scho
lastica" ("Democracy and Educational
Administration"). From *L'educazione
di oggi*. [*See 11b*] In *Il mio credo
pedagogico: Antologia dei scritti
sull'educazione*, pp. 251-66. [*See 66*]

  e. [Ital.] "Democrazia ed educazione nel mondo
contemporaneo" ("Democracy and
Education in the World of Today").

Trans. Lamberto Borghi. In *Scuola e città* (Florence), I, 8 (31 Oct. 1950), 304-8.

f. [Ital.] "Democrazia ed educazione nel mondo contemporaneo" ("Democracy and Education in the World of Today"). From *L'educazione di oggi*. [*See 11b*] In *Il mio credo pedagogico: Antologia dei scritti sull'educazione*, pp. 456-70. [*See 00*]

12. "Ethical Principles Underlying Education," *Third Yearbook*, National Herbart Society, pp. 7-34. Chicago: National Herbart Society, 1897.

a. [Bulg.] "Moral i văzpitanie," in *Učilišteto i deteto*, [pp.?]. [*See 64a*]

b. [Fren.] "Morale et éducation," in *L'école et l'enfant*, pp. 129-72. [*See 64*]

c. [Ital.] "I principii morali del processo educativo," in *Saggi pedagogici*, pp. 1-30. [*See 64b*]

d. [Kor.] [Title?] In *Hakkyo wa adong*, [pp.?] [*See 64c*]

e. [Pol.] "Zasady morale w wychowaniu," in *Szkola i dziecko*, [pp.?]. [*See 64d*]

f. [Pol.] "Zasady morale w wychowaniu," in *Szkola i dziecko*, [pp.?]. [*See 64e*]

g. [Rum.] [Title?] In *Scoala și copilul*, [pp.?]. [*See 64f*]

h. [Rum.] [Title?] In *Şcoala și copilul*, [pp.?]. [*See 64g*]

i. [Span.] "Los principios morales que cimientan la educación," in *Ensayos de educación*, pp. 1-61. [*See 65*]

13. ETHICS
    (With James H. Tufts.) New York: Henry Holt
          and Co., 1908. xii, 618 pp.
          [Rev. ed., 1932. 528 pp.]

   a. [Jap.] *Rinrigaku*. Trans. Man'ichirō Komota
            [supervised by Rikizō Nakahima; rev. by
            Yasubimi Fukusaku]. Tokyo: Kakubunkan,
            1912. 739 pp.

   b. [Jap.] *Jūi-shi gendai rinrigaku jikkō*. Trans.
            Hidehiko Miura. Tokyo: Keibunsha,
            1924. 359 pp.

   c. [Jap.] *Dyūi rinrigaku*. Trans. Hidehiko Miura.
            Tokyo: Sukia Shoin, 1927. ii, 359 pp.

   d. [Jap.] *Rinrigaku*. Trans. Riichirō Hoashi.
            Tokyo: Shunjūsha, 1962. 451 pp.
            [First Japanese trans. of the 1932 rev.
            ed.]

   e. [Urdu] *Akhlaquiyat*. Trans. Abdul-Bari Nadvi.
            Haidarabad: Jami'a-e 'Osmaniya, 1932.
            652 pp.

      Ethics [Selection(s)].
            Theory of the Moral Life, with an
            introd. by Arnold Isenberg. [Pt. II of
            the *Ethics*.] New York: Holt, Rinehart
            and Winston, 1960. 179 pp.

   f. [Hindi] *Naitik jivana ka siddhanta*. Trans.
            Krishna Chandra Mehta. Delhi: Atmaram
            and Sons, 1963. x, 168 pp.

   g. [Jap.] "Rinrigaku." Trans. Osamu Kuno. In
            Dyūi, pp. 65-198. (Sekai Dai Shisō
            Zenshū, XIX) Tokyo: Kawade Shobō,
            1960.

   h. [Port.] *Teoria de vida moral*. Trans. Leonidas
            Gontijo de Carvalho. (Clássicos da
            Democracia, XIV) São Paulo: Ibrasa,
            1964. 159 pp.

   i. [Punj.] *Sadacharek jeevan da sidhant*. Trans.
            Harbanslal Watni. Amritsar: Lok
            Sahitya Prakashan, 1966. 203 pp.

j. [Span.] *Teoría de la vida moral.* Trans.
Rafael Castillo Dibildox. México,
D.F.: Herrero Hermanos, 1944.
216 pp.

2nd[?] printing, 1965.
214 pp.

k. [Urdu] *Akhlaqi zindagi ka nazrya.* Trans. Mian
Abdur Rashid. Lahore: Maqbool Academy,
1964. 337 pp.

14. EXPERIENCE AND EDUCATION
New York: The Macmillan Co., 1938. xii, 116 pp.

a. [Arab.] *al-Khibrah wa-al-tarbiyah.* Trans.
Maḥmūd al-Basyūnī and Yūsuf Ḥammādī.
Cairo: Dār al-Ma'ārif, 1945. 100 pp.

b. [Arab.] *al-Khibrah wa-al-tarbiyah.* Trans.
Muḥammad Rif'at Ramaḍān and Najīb
Iskandar. Cairo: al-Maṭba'ah al-
Miṣrīyah, 1954. 87 pp.

c. [Bulg.] "Opităt kato osnova na obrazovanieto."
Trans. Ivan Skačokov. In *Svobodno
văzpitanie*, XVIII, 1-2 (1939-1940),
pp. 1-11; 3-4, pp. 81-94; 5-6, pp.
161-74; 7-8, pp. 241-55.

d. [Bulg.] *Opităt kato osnova na obrazovanieto.*
Trans. Ivan Skačokov. Sofia: St.
Georgiev, 1941. 60 pp.

e. [Chin.] *Ching-yen yü chiao-yü.* Trans. Hsiang-
hsü Li, *et al.* Kweiyang: Wen T'ung
Press, 1941. [pp.?]

f. [Chin.] *Ching-yen yü chiao-yü.* Trans. P'ei-yu
Li. Shanghai: The Commercial Press,
1946. [pp.?]

g. [Chin.] *Chiao-yü yü shih-yen chu-i che-hsüeh.*
Trans. Ying Hsü. Shanghai: Cheng
Chung Book Co., 1948. [pp.?]

h. [Fren.] *Expérience et éducation.* Trans. [with
an introd. by] Marie-Anne Carroi.

(Educateurs d'Hier et d'Aujourd'hui)
Paris: Bourrelier, 1947. 96 pp.

i. [Germ.] "Erfahrung und Erziehung." Trans.
Werner Correll. In *Reform des Erzie-
hungsdenkens*, pp. 27-99. Weinheim:
Verlag Julius Beltz, 1963.

j. [Greek] *Peira kai aghoki*. Trans. G. Vasdhekis.
Athens: Neon Scholeion, 1954. 88 pp.

k. [Hebr.] *Nissayon ve-hinukh*. Trans. R. Klein-
berger, [ed. A. A. Simon]. Jerusalem:
The School for Education of the Hebrew
University and the Ministry of Culture
and Education, 1960. [pp.?] [Includes
58e]

l. [Ital.] *Esperienza ed educazione*. Trans. [with
an introd. by] Ernesto Codignola.
(Educatori Antichi e Moderni, LXVI)
Florence: La Nuova Italia, 1950. xvi,
84 pp.
2nd printing, 1951
3rd printing, 1953
4th printing, 1955
5th printing, 1958
6th printing, 1960
7th printing, 1962
8th printing, 1963
9th printing, 1965
2nd edition [with corrections],
1967. xiv, 78 pp.

m. [Jap.] *Keiken to kyōiku*. Trans. Minoru
Harada. Tokyo: Shunjūsha, 1950.
139 pp.
2nd printing, 1956
3rd printing, 1961
4th printing, 1966

n. [Kor.] *Kyŏnghŏm kwa kyoyuk*. Trans. Ch'ŏn-sŏk
O. Seoul: P'ungguk Hagwŏnsa, 1947.
147 pp.

o. [Span.] *Experiencia y educación*. Trans.
Lorenzo Luzuriaga. (Biblioteca del
Maestro, I) Buenos Aires: Losada,
1939. 124 pp.

                        2nd printing, 1943
                        3rd printing, 1945.   126 pp.
                        4th printing, 1951.   116 pp.
                        5th printing, 1954.   123 pp.
                        6th printing, 1958.   125 pp.
                        7th printing, 1960
                        8th printing, 1964.   119 pp.

Experience and Education [Selection(s)].

p. [Ital.] "Esperienza ed educazione," [*see 14l*],
            Chs. III, IV, V, VII. In *Il mio credo
            pedagogico: Antologia dei scritti
            sull'educazione*, pp. 21-81. [*See 66*]

15. EXPERIENCE AND NATURE
     Chicago, London: Open Court Publishing Co., 1925.
                    ix, 443 pp.   /
                    [2nd rev. ed. New York: W. W. Norton
                    and Co., Inc., (c1929). ix, 1a-4a,
                    1-443 pp.]
                    [3rd ed. La Salle, Ill.: Open Court
                    Publishing Co., 1958. vii, xi, 360 pp.]

a. [Jap.]   *Keiken to shizen*. Trans. Riichirō
            Hoashi. Tokyo: Shunjūsha, 1959.
            377 pp.

b. [Span.] *La experiencia y la naturaleza*. Trans.
            [with an introd. by] José Gaos. México,
            D.F., Buenos Aires: Fondo de Cultura
            Económica, 1948. xxxv, 363 pp.

Experience and Nature [Selection(s)].

c. [Czech] *John Dewey: Existence, hodnota a
            kriticism*. [Ch. 10 only: "Existence,
            Value, and Criticism."] (Ruch Filoso-
            fický) Trans. Josef Schützner. Prague:
            Nákladem Překladatelů, 1925. 28 pp.

d. [Ital.] *Esperienza e natura*. Trans. [with an
            introd. and notes by] Nicola Abbagnano.
            (Collezione Bibliografica de Filosofia
            e Pedagogia) Turin, Milan: Paravia,
            1948. xxii, 163 pp.

16. FREEDOM AND CULTURE
New York: G. P. Putnam's Sons, [c1939].
176 pp.

a. [Arab.] *al-Ḥurriyah wa-al-thaqāfah*. Trans.
Amīn Mursī Qandīl. Cairo: Maktabat
al-Anjlū al-Miṣrīyah, 1955. 259 pp.

b. [Chin.] *Tzu-yu yü wen-hua*. Trans. Tsuin-chen
Ou. Taipei (Taiwan): Cheng Chung
Bookstore, 1953. 166 pp.
2nd printing, 1956

c. [Chin.] *Tzu-yu yü wen-hua*. Trans. I-liang Lin
and I-che Lou. Hong Kong: Jen-sheng
Press, 1954. 172 pp.

d. [Fren.] *Liberté et culture*. Trans. Pierre
Messiaen. (Collection Philosophie de
l'Esprit) Paris: Aubier, 1955.
191 pp.

e. [Germ.] *Mensch oder Masse*. Trans. Harry Wilcox
(J. N. Lorenz, pseud.). Vienna, Munich:
Universum Verlag, 1956. 219 pp.

f. [Greek] *Eleutheria kai politismos*. Trans. N.
Oikonomos. Athens: G. Papadhimitrious,
1955. 200 pp.

g. [Hindi] *Swantantrata aur sanskriti*. Trans.
Atmanand Vidyalankar. Allahabad:
Newspaper, Ltd., 1965. 234 pp.

h. [Ital.] *Libertà e cultura*. Trans. Enzo
Enriques Agnoletti. (Orientamenti,
Nuova Serie, XIII) Florence: La Nuova
Italia, 1953. 207 pp.
2nd printing, 1966

i. [Jap.] *Jiyū to bunka*. Trans. Takeo Hosono.
Kyoto: Hōritsu Bunka-sha, 1951.
250 pp.

j. [Kann.] *Svatantrya mattu samskritti*. Trans.
K. S. Haridasa Bhat. Udupi: Navayuga
Enterprises, 1957. viii, 188 pp.

k. [Kor.]   *Chayu wa munhwa.* Trans. Hae-yŏng Lee. Seoul: Ŭryu Munhwasa, 1954. 214 pp.

l. [Mala.]   *Svatantrayavum samskaravum.* Trans. A. N. Nambiar. Kuttipuram: Gautama Publications, 1959. 205 pp.

m. [Mara.]   *Svatantrya ani samskriti.* Trans. Ambadas S. Agnihotri. Bombay: G. P. Parchure Prakashan, 1958. 174 pp.

n. [Port.]   *Liberdade e cultura.* Trans. [with an introd. by] Eustáquio Duarte. Rio de Janeiro: Revista Branca, [n.d.]. 199 pp.
> 2nd printing, 1953. 197 pp.
>
> 3rd printing, 1956

o. [Span.]   *Libertad y cultura.* Trans. [with an introd. by] Angela Romera Vera. Rosario (Argentina): Editorial Rosario, 1946. xiv, 166 pp.

p. [Span.]   *Libertad y cultura.* Trans. Rafael Castillo Dibildox. (Manuales Uteha, número 326-326a, Sección 14, Ciencias Sociales) México, D.F.: Unión Tipográfica Editorial Hispanoamericana, 1965. 177 pp.

q. [Tamil]   *Sutantiramum panpadum.* Trans. K. S. Venkataraman. Bombay: Pearl Publications, 1958. 234 pp.

r. [Turk.]   *Özgürlük ve kültür.* Trans. Vedat Günyol. Istanbul: Katulmuş Matbassi, 1962. 167 pp.

s. [Turk.]   *Özgürlük ve kültür.* Trans. Vedat Günyol. Istanbul: Gün Basimevi, 1964. 174 pp.

Freedom and Culture [Selection(s)].

t. [Jap.]   "Ningen no jiyū no mochiikata" ("The Human Uses of Freedom") in *Jyon Dyūi; sono tetsugaku no gendai eno kiyo,* pp. 271-341. [*See 28a*]

u. [Kor.] "Chayu ŭi inganjŏk sayong," in *Dyui
sŏnjip*, pp. 267-331. [*See 28b*]

v. [Port.] [Title?] In *John Dewey, sua contribuição para a tradição americana*, [pp.?].
[*See 28c*]

17. "From Absolutism to Experimentalism," in *Contem-
porary American Philosophy: Personal Statements*.
Eds. George Plimpton Adams and William
Pepperell Montague, Vol. II, pp. 13-27.
New York: The Macmillan Co., 1930.

a. [Ital.] "Dall'assolutismo allo sperimentalismo."
Trans. Carlo Coardi. In *Filosofi
americani contemporanei*, ed. J. A.
Muirhead, pp. 117-33. (Idee Nuove, VII)
Milan: V. Bompiani, 1939.

b. [Span.] "Autobiografía filosófica." Trans.
Aníbal Sánchez Reulet[?]. In *John Dewey
en sus noventa años*, pp. 15-26. (Filosofía en América, Cuaderno no. 1)
Washington, D.C.: Pan American Union,
1949.

18. GERMAN PHILOSOPHY AND POLITICS
New York: Henry Holt and Co., 1915. 134 pp.
[2nd ed., with new foreword and introd.,
pp. 5-49. New York: G. P. Putnam's Sons,
(c1942). 149 pp.]

a. [Germ.] *Deutsche Philosophie und deutsche
Politik*. Trans. Hans Hermann Kogge
[ed. Berthold Fresow]. Meisenheim:
Westkulturverlag, A. Hain, 1954. 97 pp.
[Trans. of the 2nd ed.]

German Philosophy and Politics [Selection(s)].

b. [Jap.] "Doitsu no rekishi tetsugaku" ("The
Germanic Philosophy of History").
Trans. Takayori Iguchi. In *Warera*, I,
2 (Mar. 1919), 21-24.

19. "How Much Freedom in New Schools?" *New Republic*, LXIII (9 July 1930), 204-6.

   a. [Germ.] "Das Problem der Freiheit in den neuen Schulen," in *Der Projekt-Plan*, pp. 199-205. [*See 67*]

20. HOW WE THINK
   Boston: D. C. Heath and Co., 1910. vi, 224 pp. [Rev. ed. 1933. x, 301 pp.]

   a. [Bulg.] *Psihologija i pedagogika na misleneto*. Trans. "Bor. G." (Biblioteka Misâl i Dejnost, I) Sofia: Kjustendil, 1929. 172 pp.

   b. [Chin.] *Szu-wei shu*. Trans. Po-ming Liu. Shanghai: Chung Hua Book Co., 1921. 229 pp.
                2nd printing, [n.d.]
                3rd printing, 1933

   c. [Chin.] *Szu-hsiang fang-fa lun*. Trans. Chin-chang Ch'iu. Shanghai: World Book Co., 1935. [pp.?] [Trans. of 1933 rev. ed.]

   d. [Chin.] *Szu-wei yü chiao-hsüeh*. Trans. Hsien-ch'eng Meng and Ch'ing-t'ang Yü. Shanghai: The Commercial Press, 1936. [pp.?] [Trans. of 1933 rev. ed.]

   e. [Fren.] *Comment nous pensons*. Trans. Ovide Decroly. (Bibliothèque de Philosophie Scientifique) Paris: Ernest Flammarion, 1925. 288 pp.

   f. [Germ.] *Wie wir denken: Eine Untersuchung über die Beziehung des reflektiven Denkens zum Prozess der Erziehung*. Trans. Alice Burgeni [introd. by Leopold Deuel]. (Erkenntnis und Leben, V) Zurich: Morgartenverlag, 1951. xviii, 242 pp.

   g. [Ital.] *Come pensiamo*. Trans. [with an introd. by] Antonio Guccione-Monroy. Florence: La Nuova Italia, 1961. 423 pp.

h. [Jap.]   *Shikō no hōhō*. Trans. Seiji Ueda.
Tokyo: Shunjūsha, 1950. 306 pp.
2nd printing, 1951
3rd printing, 1956

i. [Pol.]   *Jak myślimy?* Trans. Zofja Bastgenówna
[introd. by Zygmunt Myslakowski].
(Biblioteka Przekladów Dziel Pedagogicz-
nych, XXI) Warsaw: Książka i Wiedza,
1934. xiv, 222 pp.
2nd printing, 1957. xiv,
175 pp.

j. [Port.]   *Como pensamos*. Trans. Godofredo
Rangel. (Biblioteca Pedagógica Brasileira, Atualidades Pedagógicas, II)
São Paulo: Companhia Editôra Nacional,
1933. 274 pp.
2nd printing, 1935. 276 pp.
3rd printing, [n.d.]. 249 pp.
4th printing, 1953. 242 pp.

k. [Port.]   *Como pensamos: Como se relaciona o
pensamento reflexivo com o processo
educativo*. Trans. Haydée de Camargo
Campos. (Atualidades Pedagógicas, II)
São Paulo: Companhia Editôra Nacional,
1959. 287 pp.

l. [Russ.]   *Psikhologiya i pedagogika mishleniya*.
Trans. N. M. Nikol'skii [ed. N. D.
Vinogradov]. Moscow: Mir, 1915. vi,
202 pp.
2nd printing, 1919. 196 pp.

m. [Span.]   *Como pensamos*. [Trans.?] (Ciencia y
Educación, Sección Contemporánea, Obras
de Dewey, VI) Madrid: La Lectura,
1928. 364 pp.

n. [Span.]   *Psicología del pensamiento*. Trans.
Alejandro A. Jascalevich. Boston:
D. C. Heath and Co., 1917. xxii,
247 pp.

o. [Turk.]   *Nasil Düsünürüz*. Trans. Baha Arikan,
Sabri Akdeniz, and Orhan Etker.
Istanbul: Sinan Matbaasi ve Nesriyat
Evi, 1957. 88 pp. [Selection?]

How We Think [Selection(s)].

p. [Bulg.] "Ezikat kato oradie no misalta" ("Language and the Training of Thought").
[Trans.?] In *Narodna prosveta*, I, 2
(1928), 18-24.

21. HUMAN NATURE AND CONDUCT
New York: Henry Holt and Co., 1922. vii, 336 pp.
[2nd ed., Introd. (c1930). ix, vii,
336 pp.]

a. [Arab.] *al-Ṭabī'ah al-basharīyah wa-al-sulūk
al-insānī.* Trans. Muḥammad Labīb
al-Nujayḥī. Cairo: Mu'assasat al-
Khanji, 1963. 350 pp.

b. [Germ.] *Die menschliche Natur, ihr Wesen und
ihr Verhalten.* Trans. Paul Sakmann.
Stuttgart, Berlin: Deutsche Verlags-
Anstalt, 1931. xvi, 343 pp.

c. [Hindi] *Manav prakriti aur acharan.* Trans.
Harishchandra Vidyalankar. Delhi:
Atmaram and Sons, 1963. 247 pp.

d. [Iran.] *Aklāq va shakhṣīyat.* Trans. Mochfegh
Hamadānī. Tehran: Safī-Alī-Shah,
1956. 292 pp.

e. [Ital.] *Natura e condotta dell'uomo: Intro-
duzione alla psicologia sociale.*
Trans. Giulio Preti and Aldo Visalberghi [with an introd. by Lamberto
Borghi]. (Pensatori del Nostro Tempo,
III) Florence: La Nuova Italia, 1958.
xxiv, 356 pp.
2nd printing, 1966

f. [Jap.] *Dōtoku no kaizō.* Trans. Urajirō
Imaizumi. Tokyo: Hōbunkan, 1923.
478 pp.

g. [Jap.] *Sei no ronri.* Trans. Ikutarō Shimizu.
Tokyo: Mikasa Shobō, 1938. 296 pp.

h. [Jap.] *Ningensei to kōi.* Trans. Takashi

Tōmiya. Tokyo: Shunjūsha, 1951. 275 pp.

2nd printing, 1960. 266 pp.

i. [Kor.] *Ingansŏng kwa haengwi*. Trans. Il-jeol Sire. Seoul: Sasanggye-sa, 1963. 379 pp.

j. [Port.] *A natureza humana e a conduta: Introdução à psicologia social*. Trans. Eugênio Marcondes Rocha and Jacob Thealdi. Bauru (Brazil): Tipografias e Livrarias Brazil, 1956. 259 pp.

k. [Span.] *Naturaleza humana y conducta: Introducción a la psicología social*. Trans. F. Gonzáles Aramburo. (Breviarios, CLXXVII) México, D. F.: Fondo de Cultura Económica, 1964. 308 pp.

2nd printing, 1966

l. [Swed.] *Människans natur och handlingsliv: Inledning till en social psykologi*. Trans. Alf Ahlberg. Stockholm: Natur och Kultur, 1936. iii, 275 pp.

Human Nature and Conduct [Selection(s)].

m. [Jap.] "Ningensei to kōi," in *Jyon Dyūi; sono tetsugaku no gendai eno kiyo*, pp. 238-53. [*See 28a*]

n. [Kor.] "Ingansŏng kwa haengwi," in *Dyui sŏnjip*, pp. 231-47. [*See 28b*]

o. [Port.] [Title?] In *John Dewey, sua contribuição para a tradição americana*, [pp.?]. [*See 28c*]

p. [Span.] *El hábito y el impulso en la conducta*. Trans. Dolores Cebrián[?]. (Ciencia y Educación, Sección Contemporánea, Obras de Dewey, VII) Madrid: La Lectura, 1929. 267 pp. [Contents: "El lugar del hábito en la conducta," and "El papel del impulso en la conducta."]

q. [Span.] *La inteligencia y la conducta*. Trans. Dolores Cebrián. (Ciencia y Educación,

Sección Contemporánea, Obras de Dewey,
VIII) Madrid: La Lectura, 1930. 236
pp. [Pt. III, "The Place of Intelligence in Conduct" (and Pt. IV?)]

22. IMPRESSIONS OF SOVIET RUSSIA AND THE REVOLUTION-
ARY WORLD, MEXICO--CHINA--TURKEY
New York: New Republic, Inc., 1929.
270 pp.

a. [Jap.] *Sovieto Rosha inshōki*. Trans. Tokuji
Mori. Tokyo: Jiyūsha, 1930. [pp.?]

b. [Jap.] [Title?] Trans. Fujimi Wada. In *Shin
Rosha kyōiku no hihanteki kenkyū* (*A
Critical Study of Education in the New
Russia*), by Fujimi Wada, pp. 47-124.
Tokyo: Nitto Shoin, 1930.

23. INDIVIDUALISM, OLD AND NEW
New York: Minton, Balch and Co., 1930.
171 pp.

a. [Arab.] *al-Fardīyah qadīman wa ḥadīthan.*
Trans. Khāyri Ḥammad [rev. by Marwān
al-Jābirī]. Beirut: Mu'assasat Frank-
ilīn, 1960. 156 pp.
2nd printing, [1966?]

b. [Ital.] *Individualismo vecchio e nuovo*. Trans.
[with an introd. by] Felice Villani.
(Orientamenti, XIII) Florence: La
Nuova Italia, 1948. xix, 143 pp.
2nd printing, 1949. 152 pp.

c. [Jap.] "Shinkyū kojinshugi." Trans. Kazuko
Tsurumi. In *Dyūi*, pp. 1-64. (Sekai Dai
Shisō Zenshū, XIX) Tokyo: Kawade Shobō,
1960.

Individualism, Old and New [Selection(s)].

d. [Ital.] "John Dewey: Individualismo vecchio e
nuovo." Trans. Fortunato Brancatisano.
In *Italia intellettuale*, III (Apr. 1950),
3-24.

24. "Individuality in Our Day," *New Republic*, LXII (2 Apr. 1930), 184-88.

   a. [Germ.] "Individualität in der Gegenwart." Trans. Olga Knopf. In *Internationale Zeitschrift für Individualpsychologie*, VIII (Nov.-Dec. 1930), 567-76.

25. INTELLIGENCE IN THE MODERN WORLD: John Dewey's Philosophy
Ed. [with an introd. by] Joseph Ratner. (The Modern Library.) New York: Random House, Inc., [c1939]. 1077 pp.

   a. [Chin.] *Tu-wei che-hsüeh*. Trans. I-wei Chao. Taipei (Taiwan): Ministry of Education, 1966. 2 vols. 710 pp.

26. INTEREST AND EFFORT IN EDUCATION
Boston: Houghton Mifflin Co., [c1913]. ix, 101 pp.

   a. [Arm.] [Title?] Trans. Aroos Asadian Freeman. Constantinople: Setian, 1931. [pp.?]

   b. [Bulg.] "Interesat i usilieto v obrazovanieto." Trans. Ivan Skacokov. In *Svobodno văzpitanie*, XVI, 7-8 (1937-38), 241-48; XVII, 1-2 (1938-39), 51-65; XVII, 3-4 (1938-39), 126-35; XVII, 5-6 (1938-39), 181-93; XVII, 7-8 (1938-39), 244-47.

   c. [Hebr.] "Ha-inyan veha-ma-amaz ba-hinukh." Trans. M. Segal. In *Mebifnim*, V, 1-3 (1938), 41-46; 142-51; 423-29.

   d. [Jap.] *Kyōmi to doryoku to ni motozukeru jiriki hon'i gakushū genron*. Trans. Kozue Mizuki. Tokyo: Kōtōsha, 1929. 106 pp.

   e. [Port.] "Interêsse e esfôrço." Trans. [with an introd. by] Anísio S. Teixeira [ed. Lourenço Filho]. In *Vida e educação*, Pt. II, [pp.?]. (Biblioteca de Educação, XII) São Paulo: Companhia Mel-

horamentos de São Paulo, [n.d., Pref.
1930]. [Includes 4o]
    2nd printing, [n.d.]
    3rd printing, 1952
    4th printing, [n.d.]
    5th printing, [1954?]
    6th printing, [1958?]

f. [Port.] "Interêsse e esfôrço." Trans. [with an
introd. by] Anísio S. Teixeira [ed.
Lourenço Filho.] In *Vida e educação*,
Pt. II, [pp.?]. (Biblioteca Pedagógica
Brasileira, Atualidades Pedagógicas,
LXXVI) São Paulo: Companhia Editôra
Nacional, 1959. [Includes 4p]
    2nd printing, 1962

g. [Serb.] *Sajem i usili v obrazovanie.* Trans. M.
Aerenijevic. Skoplje: Nemanja Print-
ing House, 1936. 75 pp.

h. [Span.] *El interés y el esfuerzo en la educación.*
Trans. Alfredo M. Aguayo. Havana: Edi-
torial Revista de Educación, 1925.
109 pp.

i. [Span.] *Interés y esfuerzo.* [Trans.?] Santiago
(Chile): Publicaciones de la Revista de
Educación Primaria, 1928. [pp.?] [Pub-
lished as a bulletin of the Chilean Ministry of Education.]

27. "Interest as Related to [the Training of the]
Will," in *Second Supplement to the Herbart Year-
book for 1895*, pp. 209-55. Bloomington:
(Ill.): National Herbart Society, 1896.

a. [Bulg.] "Interesät i usilieto väv vräzka s
väzpitanieto na voljata." Trans. Efr.
Beldedov. In *Učilišten pregled*, XXVII,
9-10 (1928), 1037-64.

b. [Bulg.] "Interesät i usilieto v obrazovanieto,"
in *Učilišteto i deteto*, [pp.?]. [*See
64a*]

c. [Fren.] "L'intérêt et l'effort dans leurs

rapports avec l'éducation de la volonté," in *L'école et l'enfant*, pp. 39-90. [*See 64*]

d. [Hung.] "Az érdeklödés és az eröfeszités az akaratnevelésben." Trans. Elemér Kenyeres. In *Kisdednevelés*, 9-12 (1927), 261-67, 293-97, 339-45, 374-82.

e. [Hung.] *Az érdeklödés és az eröfeszités az akaratnevelésben.* Trans. Elemér Kenyeres. Budapest: Kisdednevelés, 1927. 28 pp.

f. [Ital.] "L'interèsse in rapporto alla educazione del volere," in *Saggi pedagogici*, pp. 31-74. [*See 64b*]

g. [Kor.] [Title?] In *Hakkyo wa adong*, [pp.?]. [*See 64c*]

h. [Pol.] [Title?] In *Szkola i dziecko*, [pp.?]. [*See 64d*]

i. [Pol.] [Title?] In *Szkola i dziecko*, [pp.?]. [*See 64e*]

j. [Rum.] [Title?] In *Şcoala şi copilul*, [pp.?]. [*See 64f*]

k. [Rum.] [Title?] In *Şcoala şi copilul*, [pp.?]. [*See 64g*]

l. [Span.] "El interés en relación con el entrenamiento de la voluntad," in *Ensayos de educación*, pp. 63-100. [*See 65*]

m. [Swed.] "Om interesse och viljeansträngning." Trans. Walborg Hedberg. In *Skolan*, II (1902), [pp.?].

28. JOHN DEWEY: HIS CONTRIBUTION TO THE AMERICAN TRADITION
Ed. Irwin Edman. Indianapolis: Bobbs-Merrill Co., Inc., 1955. 322 pp.
[Contents: *Reconstruction in Philosophy*, Chs. I, IV, VIII.

Democracy and Education, parts of Chs.
 I-XII, XVIII-XX, XXIV, XXVI.
Human Nature and Conduct, parts of Pts.
 I, II, III.
Logic: The Theory of Inquiry, parts of
 Chs. II, VI.
Freedom and Culture, Chs. I, II, VII.
A Common Faith, parts of Chs. II, III.
"Creative Democracy--The Task Before
 Us."]

a. [Jap.] *Jyon Dyūi; sono tetsugaku no gendai eno
 kiyo*. Trans. Masako Shoji, Tsuguo Doi,
 and Hisao Kamidera. Tokyo: Tōkō Shoin,
 1961. 368 pp.

b. [Kor.] *Dyui sŏnjip*. Trans. Ch'ŏn-sŏk O.
 Seoul: Ŭryu Munhwasa, 1957. 361 pp.

c. [Port.] *John Dewey, sua contribuição para a
 tradição americana*. Trans. Stella C. L.
 Tostes. (Biblioteca Fundo Universal de
 Cultura, Estante de Pedagogia) Rio de
 Janeiro: Fundo de Cultura, 1960. 339 pp.

29. THE JOHN DEWEY REPORT
 Ankara: Research and Measurement Bureau of the
 Ministry of Education, 1960. 27 pp.
 [First English publication, from type-
 script of original prepared by Dewey
 in 1924.]

a. [Turk.] *Türkiye maarifi hafkinda rapor (Report
 and Recommendation upon Turkish Education)*. [Trans.?] Istanbul: Devlet
 Basimevi, 1939. vi, 30 pp.

b. [Turk.] *Türkiye maarifi hafkinda rapor (Report
 and Recommendation upon Turkish Education)*. [Trans.?] Ankara: Millî
 Eğitim Bakanliği, Talim ve Terbiye
 Dairesi Test ve Araştirma Bürosu, 1952.
 30 pp.

30. LIBERALISM AND SOCIAL ACTION
New York: G. P. Putnam's Sons [c1935].
viii, 93 pp.

a. [Ital.] *Liberalismo e azione sociale*. Trans.
R. Cresti. (Orientamenti, Nuova Serie,
III) Florence: La Nuova Italia, 1946.
120 pp.
2nd printing, 1948. xii,
116 pp.
3rd printing, 1962. viii,
116 pp.
4th printing, 1965
5th printing, 1968

b. [Jap.] "Jivūshigi to shakai kōdō." Trans.
Yūjirō Nakamura. In *Dyūi*, pp. 249-304.
(Sekai Dai Shisō Zenshū, XIX) Tokyo:
Kawade Shobō, 1960.

31. THE LIVING THOUGHTS OF THOMAS JEFFERSON
New York: Longmans, Green and Co., 1940. 173 pp.

a. [Arab.] *Ārā' Tūmās Jifirsūn al-ḥayyah*. Trans.
Maḥmūd Yūsuf Zāyid [rev. by Jibrā'īl
Jabbūr]. Beirut: Dār al-Thaqāfah,
1957. 260 pp.

b. [Arab.] *Jifirsūn*. Trans. 'Abd al-Hamīd Yūnūs
[rev. by 'Alī Ad'ham]. Cairo: Dār
al-Fikr al-'Arabi, 1961. 201 pp.

c. [Indo.] *Pirikan Thomas Jefferson*. Trans. Suwarno
Hadiatmodjo. Djakarta: Endang, 1963.
173 pp.

d. [Ital.] *Thomas Jefferson: Presentato da John
Dewey*. Trans. Georgia Monoicelli.
Milan: Mondadori, 1952. 145 pp.

e. [Port.] *O pensamento vivo de Jefferson*. Trans.
Lêda Bolchart Rodrigues. (Biblioteca
do Pensamento Vivo, XII) São Paulo:
Livraria Martins, [n.d.]. 226 pp.
2nd printing, 1942. 204 pp.
3rd printing, 1952. 208 pp.

f. [Span.] *El pensamiento vivo de Jefferson.*
Trans. Luis Echávarri. (Biblioteca del
Pensamiento Vivo, XXVI) Buenos Aires:
Losada, 1944. 224 pp.
2nd printing, 1950. 226 pp.
3rd printing, 1959. 224 pp.

32. "The Logic of Judgments of Practice," *Journal of
Philosophy* [*Psychology, and Scientific Methods*],
XII (16 Sept. 1915), 505-23.

a. [Czech] *Logika soudů praktických, zejména
hodnotních.* Trans. Josef Schützner.
(Ruch Filosofický) Prague: Nákladem
Prekladatelů, 1926. 30 pp.

33. LOGIC: THE THEORY OF INQUIRY
New York: Henry Holt and Co., [c1938].
viii, 546 pp.

a. [Arab.] *al-Manṭiq: Naẓarīyat al-baḥth.* Trans.
Zakī Najīb Maḥmūd. Cairo: Dār al-
Ma'ārif, 1960. 855 pp.
2nd printing, [1963?]

b. [Fren.] *Logique: La théorie de l'enquête.*
Trans. [with an introd. by] Gérard
Deledalle. (Publications de la
Faculté des Lettres et Sciences
Humaines de Tunis, 6th series: "Phi-
losophie," II) Paris: Presses Uni-
versitaires de France, 1966. 696 pp.

c. [Ital.] *Logica, teoria dell'indagine.* Trans.
[with an introd. by] Aldo Visalberghi.
(Biblioteca de Cultura Filosofica, II)
Turin: G. Einaudi, 1949. 700 pp.
2nd printing, 1965

d. [Serb.] *Logika: Teorija istraživanja.* Trans.
Vasilije Tomović [with an introd. by
Miladin Životić]. Belgrade: Nolit,
1962. 533 pp.

e. [Span.] *Lógica: Teoría de la investigación.*

Trans. [with an introd. by] Eugenio
Imaz. México, D.F., Buenos Aires:
Fondo de Cultura Económica, 1950. xxx,
599 pp.

Logic: The Theory of Inquiry [Selection(s)].

f. [Jap.] "Chisei to tankyū" ("Intelligence and
Inquiry") in *Jyon Dyūi; sono tetsugaku
no gendai eno kiyo*, pp. 254-70. [*See
28a*]

g. [Kor.] "Chisŏng kwa t'amgu," in *Dyui sŏnjip*,
pp. 249-65. [*See 28b*]

h. [Port.] [Title?] In *John Dewey, sua contribuição para a tradição americana*, [pp.?].
[*See 28c*]

34. MESSAGE TO THE CHINESE PEOPLE
Typewritten manuscript in the National Archives,
Washington, D.C., [1942?]. 3 pp.

a. [Chin.] *Tu-wei po-shih kao Chung-kuo jen-min
shu.* [Trans.?] Washington, D.C.:
[Office of War Information?], 1942.
7 pp.

35. MORAL PRINCIPLES IN EDUCATION
Boston: Houghton Mifflin Co., [c1909].
ix, 60 pp.

a. [Arab.] *al-Mabādi' al-Akhlāqiyah fī al-tarbiyah.*
Trans. 'Abd al-Fattāḥ al-Sayyid Hilāl
[rev. by Aḥmad Fu'ād al-Ahwānī]. Cairo:
al-Dār al'Miṣrīyah lil-Ta'līf wa-al-
Tarjamah wa-al-Nashr, 1966. 140 pp.

b. [Bulg.] "Moral i văzpitanie." Trans. "B." In
Učilišten pregled, XXII, 6 (1923),
315-38.

c. [Chin.] *Te-yü yüan-li.* Trans. Hsiang-jen Wen.
Shanghai: Chung Hua Book Co., [n.d.].
[pp.?]

d. [Czech] *Mravní zásady ve vychové*. Trans. F. Pavlásek [with a preface by Miloslav Skořepa]. Prague: Dědictiví Komenskeho, 1934. 32 pp.

e. [Jap.] "Kyōiku niokeru dōtoku-teki genri." Trans. Yoshiaki Matsuda. In *Dōtoku kyōiku no kenkyū* by Yoshiaki Matsµda, pp. 93-131. Tokyo: Meigen Shobō, 1961.

f. [Pol.] *Zasady moralne w wychowaniu*. Trans. Witold Hofman. Lvov: Wyd. Zakl. Nar. im Ossolińskich, 1921. 39 pp.

g. [Turk.] *Terbiyede ahlâk prensipleri*. Trans. Belkis Halim. Istanbul: Hüsnütabiat Basimevi, 1934. 55 pp.

36. "My Pedagogic Creed," *School Journal*, LIV (16 Jan. 1897), 77-80.

a. [Arab.] [Title?] Trans. Aḥmad Fu'ād al-Ahwānī. In *John Dewey*, by Aḥmad Fu'ād al-Ahwānī. Cairo: Dār al-Ma'ārif 1959, [pp.?].

b. [Chin.] *Wo-ti chiao-yü hsin-t'iao*. Trans. Chiu-sam Tsang. Hong Kong: Progressive Education Press, 1959. [pp.?]

c. [Chin.] *Wo chih chiao-yü chu-i*. Trans. Tsunghai Cheng. Shanghai: The Commercial Press, [n.d.]. [pp.?]

d. [Fren.] "Mon credo pédagogique." Trans. Tsuin-chen Ou. In *La doctrine pédagogique de John Dewey* by Tsuin-chen Ou, pp. 255-72. Paris: Les Presses Modernes, 1931.

e. [Fren.] "Mon credo pédagogique." Trans. Tsuin-chen Ou. In *La doctrine pédagogique de John Dewey* by Tsuin-chen Ou, pp. 255-72. (Bibliothèque d'Histoire de la Philosophie) Paris: J. Vrin, 1958.

f. [Germ.] [Title?] Trans. Rudolf Prantl. In
*Zeitschrift für christliche Erziehungs-
wissenschaft und Schulpolitik*, XV
(1925), 465-76.

g. [Hebr.] *Ani ma'amin be-hinukh*. Trans. Yitzchak
Mann. (Shviley Hinukh) Merchavia:
Sifriat Hapoalim, 1964. 45 pp.

h. [Ital.] *Il mio credo pedagogico*. Trans. Luigi
Oliva. Rome: Unione Editrice, 1913.
25 pp.

i. [Ital.] "Il mio credo pedagogico," in *L'educazione di oggi*, pp. 3-18. [*See 11b*]

j. [Ital.] "Il mio credo pedagogico," in *Il mio
credo pedagogico: Antologia dei scritti
sull'educazione*, pp. 3-31. [*See 66*]

k. [Jap.] *Kyōiku shinjō*. Trans. Mitsuo Kodama.
Tokyo: Shunjūsha, 1950. 20 pp.
2nd printing, 1956
3rd printing, 1961
4th printing, 1966

l. [Jap.] "Kyōiku shinjō." Trans. Tsunekichi
Mizuno. In *Dyūi kyōiku shisō kenkyū
no tebiki* by Tsunekichi Mizuno, pp.
11-42. Tokyo: Risōsha, 1959.

m. [Pol.] "Moje pedagogiczne credo." Trans. Jozef
Pieter. In *Skola a spoleczeństwo*, [pp.?].
[*See 53x*]

n. [Span.] "Mi credo pedagógico." Trans. J. Paulău
Vera. In *Quaderns d'estudi*, (Nov. 1917
and Jan. 1918), [pp.?]. [Catalan?]

o. [Span.] "Mi credo pedagógico," in *Ensayos de
educación*, pp. 129-34. [*See 65*]

p. [Span.] "Mi credo pedagógico." Trans. Lorenzo
Luzuriaga. In *Revista de pedagogía*,
[Madrid], X, 109 (Jan. 1931), 1-5; X,
110 (Feb. 1931), 74-80.

q. [Span.] "Mi credo pedagógico." [Trans.?] In
Revista de educación, [Santiago, Chile],
(Nov. 1949), [pp.?].

r. [Span.] "Mi credo pedagógico." Trans. Darío E. Salas. In *Boletín de la Secretaria de Educación Pública*, [Tegucigalpa, Honduras], I, 3 (Jan.-Mar. 1950), 2-6.

s. [Span.] "Mi credo pedagógico." Trans. Darío E. Salas. In *Cultura*, [Tegucigalpa, Honduras], (Jan.-Feb. 1950), 15-27.

t. [Span.] "Mi credo pedagógico." Trans. Darío E. Salas. In *Nueva educación*, [Lima, Peru], (Mar. 1950), 3-11.

u. [Span.] "Mi credo pedagógico," in *El niño y el programa escolar. Mi credo pedagógico*, [pp.?] [*See 4v*]

37. "The Need for a Recovery of Philosophy," in *Creative Intelligence*, pp. 3-69. New York: Henry Holt and Co., [c1917].

a. [Ital.] *Intelligenza creativa*. Trans. [with an introd. by] Lamberto Borghi. (Pensatori Antichi e Moderni, LI) Florence: La Nuova Italia, (Mar.) 1957. iv, 120 pp.
  2nd printing, (Oct.) 1957
  3rd printing, 1962. iv, 116 pp.
  4th printing, 1965
  5th printing, 1967

b. [Jap.] *Tetsugaku no kakushin*. Trans. Yoshio Nagano. Tokyo: Kyōiku Gakujutsu Kai, 1936. [pp.?]

c. [Jap.] "Sōzōteki chisei." Trans. Ikutarō Shimizu. In *Sōzōteki chisei*, by Ikutarō Shimizu, pp. 1-75. Tokyo: Kawade Shobō, 1936.
  2nd printing, 1941

38. "New Schools for a New Era," *New Republic*, LVII (12 Dec. 1928), 91-94.

a. [Span.] "Escuelas nuevas." [Trans.?] In

Coopera, [México, D.F.: Revista de
Educación], No. 10 (July-Aug. 1929),
519-22.

39. "The Objectivism-Subjectivism of Modern Philos-
    ophy," *Journal of Philosophy*, XXXVIII (25 Sept.
    1941), 533-42.

    a. [Ital.] "L'oggettivismo-soggettivismo della
       filosofia moderna." Trans. Aldo Visal-
       berghi. In *Rivista di filosofia*,
       [Milan], XLI, 1 (Jan.-Mar. 1950), 59-72.

    b. [Ital.] "L'oggettivismo-soggettivismo della
       filosofia moderna." Trans. Aldo Visal-
       berghi. In *Problemi di tutti*, [pp.?].
       [*See 44b*]

40. OUTLINES OF A CRITICAL THEORY OF ETHICS
    Ann Arbor: Register Publishing Co., 1891.
    viii, 253 pp.

    a. [Jap.] "Deuē-shi rinrigaku koyo." Trans.
       Tokuzō Nakajima. In *Zoho kaitei rin-
       rigakusho kaisetsu* by Tokuzō Nakajima,
       pp. 519-646. Tokyo: Ikuseikai, 1900.
       [A summary trans. with commentary.]

41. PHILOSOPHY AND CIVILIZATION
    New York: Minton, Balch and Co., 1931. vii,
    334 pp.

    a. [Pol.] *Filozofia a cywilizacja*. Trans. Stefan
       Purman. Warsaw: J. Przeworski, 1938.
       342 pp.

42. THE PHILOSOPHY OF JOHN DEWEY
    Ed. Joseph Ratner. New York: Henry Holt and
    Co., [c1928]. xii, 560 pp.

    a. [Span.] *Pedagogía y filosofía*. Trans. J. Méndes

Herrera. (Biblioteca Moderna de Filosofía y Ciencias Sociales) Madrid:
F. Beltrán, 1930. 558 pp.

43. "The Pragmatism of Peirce," *Journal of Philosophy*, XIII (21 Dec. 1916), 709-15.

   a. [Ital.] "Il pragmatismo di Peirce." Trans.
Nicola and Maria Abbagnano. In *Caso,
amore, e logica* by Charles Santiago S.
Peirce, pp. 301-8. Turin: Taylor,
1956.

44. PROBLEMS OF MEN
New York: Philosophical Library, [c1946]. 424 pp.
[Abridged ed., *Philosophy of Education*.
Ames (Iowa): Littlefield, Adams and Co.,
1956. 311 pp.]

   a. [Hindi] *Shiksha darshan ki bhumika*. Trans.
Surendrapala Simha. Allahabad: Bharati
Bhandar, 1957. 520 pp. [Trans. of the
abridged ed.]

   b. [Ital.] *Problemi di tutti*. Trans. Giulio Preti.
(Il Pensiero Critico, XVII) Milan:
Mondadori, 1950. x, 500 pp.

   c. [Span.] *El hombre y sus problemas*. Trans.
Eduardo Prieto. (Biblioteca del Hombre
Contemporáneo) Buenos Aires: Paidós,
1952. 363 pp.
                2nd printing, 1961. 243 pp.

Problems of Men [Selection(s)].

   d. [Russ.] *Filosofstvuyushchie*. Trans. G. Alek-
sandrov. Moscow: Pravda, 1947.
38 pp.

45. "Progressive Education and the Science of Education," *Progressive Education*, V (July-Aug.-Sept.
1928), 197-204.

a. [Bulg.] "Progresivnoto obrazovanie i pedagogi-
českata nauka." Trans. G. D. Pir'ov.
In *Svobodno vâzpitanie*, VII, 5-6 (1928-
29), 142-49.

46. PSYCHOLOGY
New York: Harper and Brothers, 1887 [c1886].
xii, 417 pp.

a. [Jap.] *Deuě no shinrigaku*. Trans. Yōhei
Nishiyama. Tokyo: Yūbunkaku, 1931.
viii, 306 pp.

47. "Psychology and Social Practice," *Psychological
Review*, VII (Mar. 1900), 105-24. [Abstract,
127-28.]
Science, XI (2 Mar. 1900), 321-33.

a. [Span.] "La psicología y la práctica social,"
in *Ensayos de educación*, pp. 135-74.
[*See 65*]

48. THE PSYCHOLOGY OF NUMBER AND ITS APPLICATIONS TO
METHODS OF TEACHING ARITHMETIC
(with James A. McLellan). (International Education Series, ed. William Torrey
Harris, XXXIII) New York: D. Appleton
and Co., 1895. xv, 309 pp.

a. [Jap.] *Sansū shinrigaku*. Trans. Kitarō Nishiyama. Tokyo: Seiundō, 1902. 346 pp.

49. THE PUBLIC AND ITS PROBLEMS
New York: Henry Holt and Co. [c1927].
vi, 224 pp.

a. [Span.] *El público y sus problemas*. Trans.
Mario H. Calicchio. (Colección Hombres
y Problemas, XVI) Buenos Aires: Editorial Agora, 1958. 173 pp.

50. THE QUEST FOR CERTAINTY
    New York: Minton, Balch and Co., 1929.
    318 pp.

a. [Arab.] *al-Baḥth 'an al-yaqīn*. Trans. Aḥmad
Fu'ād al-Ahwānī. Cairo: 'Īsā al-Bābī
al-Ḥalabī, 1960. 342 pp.

b. [Greek] *I anazitissi tis vevaiotitas*. Trans.
Manoles Kornelios. Athens: Ikaros,
1957. 280 pp.
2nd printing, 1959

c. [Ital.] *La ricerca della certezza: Studio sul
rapporto tra conoscenza e azione*.
Trans. Egle Becchi and Alfredo Rizzardi
[with an introd. by Aldo Visalberghi].
Florence: La Nuova Italia, 1966. xiv,
336 pp.

d. [Jap.] *Kakujitsusei no tankyū: Chishiki to
kōki to no kankei no ichikosatsu*.
Trans. Seiji Ueda. Tokyo: Risōsha,
1935. 373 pp.

e. [Jap.] *Kakujitsu no tankyū*. Trans. Seiji
Ueda. Tokyo: Shunjūsha, 1950. 386 pp.
2nd printing, Nov. 1950
3rd printing, 1951
4th printing [rev. by Seiji
Ueda], 1963. 386 pp.

f. [Span.] *La busca de la certeza: Un estudio de
la relación entre el conocimiento y la
acción*. Trans. [with an introd. by]
Eugenio Imaz. (Obras de Filosofía)
México, D.F., Buenos Aires: Fondo de
Cultura Económica, 1952. xviii, 275 pp.

51. RECONSTRUCTION IN PHILOSOPHY
    New York: Henry Holt and Co., 1920. vii,
    224 pp.
    [Enlarged ed., with a new introd. by
    the author. Boston: The Beacon Press,
    (c1948). xlvii, 224 pp.]

a. [Arab.] *al-Tajdīd fi al-falsafah*. Trans. Amīn

Mursī Qandīl [rev. by Zakī Najīb Maḥ-
mūd]. Cairo: Maktabat al-Anjlū al-
Miṣrīyah, 1957. 340 pp.

b. [Chin.] *Che-hsüeh chih kai tsao*. Trans. Ch'ung-
ch'ing Hsü. Changsha (China): The
Commercial Press, 1939. 174 pp.
2nd printing, [Taipei
(Taiwan)] 1966

c. [Chin.] *Che-hsüeh ti kai-tsao*. Trans. Shih Hu
and Yüeh T'ang. Taipei (Taiwan): Wen
Hsing Bookstore, (Jan.) 1965. 2 vols.
201 pp.
2nd printing, (June) 1965

d. [Czech] *Rekonstrukce ve filosofii*. Trans.
Josef Schützner. (Škola Vševědná,
XXIV) Prague: Sfinx, 1929. 211 pp.

e. [Iran.] *Bonyad-e now dar falsafah*. Trans.
S. A. Saeedi. Tehran: Eqbal, 1958.
172 pp.

f. [Ital.] *Ricostruzione filosòfica*. Trans. [with
an introd. by] Guido de Ruggiero.
(Bibliografico di Cultura Moderna)
Bari: Laterza and Figli, 1931.
215 pp.

g. [Jap.] *Tetsugaku no kaizō*. Trans. Meikichi
Chiba. Tokyo: Dōbunkan, 1921.
424 pp.

h. [Jap.] *Tetsugaku no kaizō*. Trans. Shin'ichi
Nakajima. Tokyo: Iwanami Shoten,
1921. 232 pp.
2nd printing, 1924

i. [Jap.] *Tetsugaku no kaizō*. Trans. Kokusaburō
Nieda. Tokyo: Shunjūsha, 1950.
160 pp.

j. [Kor.] *Ch'ŏrhak ŭi kaejo*. Trans. Pŏm-mo
Chŏng. Seoul: Ŭryu Munhwasa, 1960.
195 pp.

k. [Mala.] *Tatwa vignanthil punarnirmanam*. Trans.
K. M. George. Kottayam: Sahtiya

Pravertaka Cooperative Society, 1955.
213 pp.

l. [Port.] *A filosofia em reconstrução*. Trans.
Eugênio Marcondes Rocha. (Biblioteca
Universitária, Filosofia e Lógica, I)
São Paulo: Companhia Editôra Nacional,
1958. xiii, 205 pp.

m. [Port.] *Reconstrução em filosofia*. Trans.
Antonio Pinto de Carvalho [rev. by
Anísio S. Teixeira]. (Biblioteca Universitária, Filosofia, I) São Paulo:
Companhia Editôra Nacional, 1959.
224 pp. [This edition . . . "publicada
sob os auspícios do Instituto Nacional /
de Estudos Pedagógicos do Ministério da
Educação e Cultura, em comemoração do
centenário do nascimento de John Dewey."]

n. [Span.] *Reconstrucción de la filosofía*. Trans.
Domingo Barnés. (Ciencia y Educación,
Sección Contemporánea, Obras de Dewey,
VIII) Madrid: La Lectura, 1930.
272 pp.

o. [Span.] *La reconstrucción de la filosofía*.
Trans. Amando Lázaro Ros [with an
introd. by Luis Rodríguez Aranda].
(Biblioteca de Iniciación Filosófica,
XXXVII) Buenos Aires: Aguilar, 1955.
277 pp.
                    2nd printing, 1959.   283 pp.
                    3rd printing, 1964.   279 pp.

p. [Tamil] *Tattuva sattiram punaramaippu*. Trans.
A. S. Jnanasambandhan. Madras: Pri-
vate Books of India, 1957.   206 pp.

Reconstruction in Philosophy [Selection(s)].

q. [Germ.] "Vom Ursprung des Philosophierens:
Philosophie im Wandel der Auffassun-
gen." [Trans.?] [Ch. 1, "Changing
Conceptions of Philosophy."] In *Der
Monat*, II, 13 (Oct. 1949), 25-35.

r. [Ital.] *Ricostruzione della filosofia*. Trans.
Giorgio Tagliacozzo. Rome: United

States Information Service, 1951-52.
[Trans. of the Introd. to the 1930 ed.,
first presented over the Voice of
America in four sections:

   I. 9 Feb. 1951: "Ricostruzione
        della filosofia." 4 pp.
  II. 27 Apr. 1951: "Scienza e filo-
        sofia." 4 pp.
 III. 5 Oct. 1951: "Il compito della
        filosofia." 4 pp.
  IV. Jan. 1952. "Verso un'etica
        moderna." 4 pp.]

s. [Ital.]   "Scienza e filosofia." Trans. Giorgio
Tagliacozzo. In *Minerva (Rivista delle
Riviste)*, XVI, 7 (July 1951), 219-22.
[*See 51rII*]

t. [Ital.]   "Ricostruzione della filosofia." Trans.
Guido de Ruggiero. In *Il pensiero
moderno in America*, pp. 77-103. Turin:
Edizioni Radio Italiana, 1955. [*See
51r*]

u. [Jap.]   "Keiken oyobi risei no gainen no henka."
Trans. Shin'ichi Nakajima. [Ch. IV,
"Changing Conceptions of Experience and
Reason."] In *Tetsugaku zasshi*, XXXIV,
388 (1 June 1919), 57-78.

v. [Jap.]   "Tetsugaku no kaizō," in *Jyon Dyūi;
sono tetsugaku no gendai eno kiyo*,
pp. 22-87. [*See 28a*]

w. [Kor.]   "Ch'ŏrhak ŭi kaejo," in *Dyui sŏnjip*,
pp. 33-93. [*See 28b*]

x. [Port.]   [Title?] In *John Dewey, sua contribuição para a tradição americana*,
[pp.?]. [*See 28c*]

52.   "The Rôle of Philosophy in the History of
Civilization," *Philosophical Review*, XXXVI
(Jan. 1927), 1-9.

a. [Czech]   *Úloha filosofie v dějinách civilisace.*
Trans. Josef Schützner. Prague:

Nákladem Vlastním, 1927. 8 pp.

53. THE SCHOOL AND SOCIETY
    Chicago: University of Chicago Press, 1899.
    125 pp.
    [2nd ed., 1900. 129 pp.]
    [Rev. ed., 1915. xv, 164 pp.]

    a. [Arab.] *wa-al-mujtama'*. Trans.
       Dīmītrī Qandilaft [with an introd. by
       R. Galt]. Cairo: Maṭba'at al-Ma'ārif,
       1928. 209 pp.

    b. [Arab.] [Title?] Trans. Ahmad Hassan al-Rahīm.
       Beirut: Dār al-Haẏat Press, 1964.
       [pp.?]

    c. [Bulg.] [Title?] Trans. Dobroslav Miletic.
       Sofia: [n.p.], 1935. [pp.?] /

    d. [Bulg.] *Učilisteto i obštestvoto*. [Trans.?]
       (Biblioteka Dom i Učilište, XI) Sofia:
       Hudožnik, 1940. 32 pp.

    e. [Czech] *Škola a společnost*. Trans. Ján Mrazík.
       (Otázky a Názory, X) Prague: J.
       Laichter, 1904. 99 pp.

    f. [Dutch] *School en maatschappij*. Trans. Tjitze
       J. deBoer. (Bekende Paedagogen)
       Groningen: J. B. Wolters, 1929. viii,
       218 pp.

    g. [Finn.] *Koulu ja yhteiskunta*. Trans. Kalevi
       Kajava. (Otavan Filosofinen Kirjasto,
       V) Helsinki: Otava, 1957. 154 pp.
       [Trans. of the rev. ed., 1915.]

    h. [Germ.] *Schule und öffentliches Leben*. Trans.
       Elsie Gurlitt [with an introd. by Lud-
       wig Gurlitt]. Berlin: Walter, 1905.
       vi, 72 pp.

    i. [Hebr.] "Beit ha-sefer veha-hevrah." Trans.
       Haim Braver [with an introd. by P. A.
       Kleinberger]. In *Ha-yeled ve-tokhnit
       ha-limudim*, [pp.?]. Tel-Aviv: Otzar
       Hamoreh, 1960. [Includes 4h]

j. [Hung.] *Az iskola és a társadalom*. Trans.
Frigyes Ozorai. (Néptanitók Könyvtára,
XLV) Budapest: Lampel, 1912. 77 pp.

k. [Iran.] *Madreseh va jame-êh*. Trans. Mochfegh
Hamadānī. Tehran: Safī-Alī-Shah, 1948.
123 pp.

1. [Ital.] *La scuola e la società*. Trans. Guis-
sepina di Laghi. Catania: F. Battiato,
1915. 92 pp.

m. [Ital.] *Scuola e società*. Trans. Ernesto Codignola and Lamberto Borghi [with an in-
trod. by Ernesto Codignola]. (Educatori
Antichi e Moderni, LXV) Florence: La
Nuova Italia, 1949. xx, 140 pp.
[Trans. of the rev. ed.]
2nd printing, 1950
3rd printing, (Jan.) 1951
4th printing, (Nov.) 1951
5th printing, 1952
6th printing, 1953
7th printing, (Feb.) 1954
8th printing, (Dec.) 1954
9th printing, 1956
10th printing, 1957
11th printing, 1958
12th printing, 1959
13th printing, (Mar.) 1961
14th printing, (Nov.) 1961
15th printing, 1962
16th printing, 1963
17th printing, (Feb.) 1964
18th printing, (May) 1964
19th printing, 1965
20th printing, ["New Ed."]
(Feb.) 1967. xviii,
130 pp.
21st printing, (Sept.) 1967

n. [Jap.] *Gakkō to shakai*. Trans. Yōichi Ueno
[rev. by Tarō Tominaga]. Tokyo:
Matsumuro Sanshōdō, 1901. 105 pp.

o. [Jap.] *Gakkō to shakai*. Trans. Koreichiro
Baba. Tokyo: Nihon Shoseki Kabushiki
Kaisha, 1905. [pp.?] [Commissioned by
the Ministry of Education as a teaching
guidebook.]

p. [Jap.] "Gakkō to shakai." Trans. Sajū Tasei. In *Tetsugaku to kyōiku: Gakkō to shakai*, ed. Sajū Tasei, pp. 251-450. Tokyo: Bunkyō Shoin, 1925. [Includes a trans. of Paul Natorp's *Philosophy and Education*.]

q. [Jap.] "Gakkō to shakai." Trans. Sajū Tasei. In *Tetsugaku to kyōiku: Gakkō to shakai*. Osaka: Osaka Hōbunkan, 1925. [*See 53p*]

r. [Jap.] *Gakkō to shakai*. Trans. Yorio Tayori. Tokyo: Sekai Kyōiku Bunko Kankōkai, 1935. vii, 141 pp.

s. [Jap.] *Gakkō to shakai*. Trans. [with a commentary] by Seiichi Miyahara. Tokyo: Shunjūsha, 1950. 158 pp.
        2nd printing, 1954
        3rd printing, 1957
        4th printing, 1959

t. [Jap.] *Gakkō to shakai*. Trans. [with a commentary by] Seiichi Miyahara. Tokyo: Iwanami Shoten, 1957. 158 pp.

u. [Kor.] *Hakkyo wa sahoe*. Trans. Chŏng-dŏk Kang. Seoul: Chŏngŭmsa, 1947. 117 pp.

v. [Lat.] *Škola un sabīdrība*. Trans. P. Baško. Riga, (Latvian S.S.R.): Izgleitība, 1926. 54 pp.

w. [Pol.] *Skola a spoleczeństwo*. Trans. Marja Lisowska. Lvov: Książnica Polska, 1924. 101 pp.

x. [Pol.] *Skola a spoleczeństwo*. Trans. Róża Czaplińska-Mutermilchowa. (Biblioteka Przekladów Dziel Pedagogiczynch, I) Lvov, Warsaw: Książnica-Atlas, 1933. [pp.?] [Includes *36m*]

y. [Russ.] *Shkola i obschestvo*. Trans. I. I. Gorbunov-Posadov. (Svobodnoe Vospitanie i Obrazovanie, XI) Moscow: Mosrednik, 1907. 60 pp.

z. [Russ.] *Shkola i obschestvo*. Trans. I. I. Gorbunov-Posadov. (Padagogicheskaya

Biblioteka, I) Kaluga: Kooperativ
Uchashchiksya, 1920. 40 pp.

aa. [Russ.] *Shkola i obschestvo*. Trans. [with an
introd. by] S. T. Shatskii. Moscow:
Rabotnik Prosveshcheniya, 1922. 48 pp.
2nd printing, 1923. 46 pp.

bb. [Russ.] *Shkola i obschestvo*. Trans. [with an
introd. by] G. A. Luchinskii. (Peda-
gogicheskaya Biblioteka, X) Moscow:
Gosizdat, 1924. 175 pp.
2nd printing, 1925. 127 pp.

cc. [Serb.] *Skola i obshchestvo*. Trans. N. Vanlic.
Belgrade: Rajković Bookshop, 1935.
Pt. I, 32 pp.; Pt. II, 32 pp.

dd. [Span.] *La escuela y la sociedad*. Trans.
Lorenzo Luzuriaga. Madrid: Francisco
Beltrán, 1900. [pp.?]

ee. [Span.] *La escuela y la sociedad*. Trans. [with
an introd. by] Domingo Barnés. (Libre-
ría Española y Extranjera, Actualidades
Pedagógicas) Madrid: Francisco Beltrán,
1921. 135 pp. [Trans. of the 1899 ed.]
2nd printing, 1925
3rd printing, 1929. 132 pp.

ff. [Turk.] *Mektep ve cemiyet*. Trans. Başman Avni.
Istanbul: Türkiye Cumhuriyeti Maarif
Vekâleti, 1924. 104 pp.

gg. [Turk.] *Mektep ve cemiyet*. Trans. Başman Avni.
Istanbul: Devlet Matbassi, 1930.
277 pp.

The School and Society [Selection(s)].

hh. [Fren.] "L'école et le progrès social." Trans.
J. Desfeuille. In *L'éducation*, I (Mar.
1909), 198-217.

ii. [Fren.] "L'école et la vie de l'enfant."
Trans. J. Desfeuille. In *L'éducation*,
IV, 4 (Dec. 1912), 457-72.

jj. [Fren.] [Title?] ["Waste in Education."]

Trans. Henri Marty. In *L'éducation*,
(June 1914), [pp.?].

kk. [Ital.] "La scuola e il progresso sociale,"
[from *Scuola e società* (*See 53m*)]. In
*Il mio credo pedagogico: Antologia dei
scritti sull'educazione*, pp. 32-58.
[*See 66*]
"La scuola e la vita del fanciullo,"
[from *Scuola e società* (*See 53m*)]. In
*Il mio credo pedagogico: Antologia dei
scritti sull'educazione*, pp. 23-44.
[*See 66*]
"Psicologia dell'istruzione elementare,"
[from *Scuola e società* (*See 53m*)]. In
*Il mio credo pedagogico: Antologia dei
scritti sull'educazione*, pp. 69-87.
[*See 66*]

11. [Swed.] *Skolan och samhället.* Pt. I: "Skolan
och det sociala framåtskridandet" ("The
School and Social Progress"), pp. 53-67.
Pt. II: "Skolan och barnets lif" ("The
School and the Life of the Child"), pp.
95-108. Trans. Walborg Hedberg. In
*Skolan: Tidskrift till främjande af de
allmänna läroverkens tidsenliga utveck-
ling*, II (1902).

mm. [Swed.] *Skolan och samhället.* Trans. Walborg
Hedberg. [Extract] in *Källor till
uppfostrans och pedagogiska reformidéernas historia*, by B. R. Hall, pp. 138-50.
Stockholm: P. A. Norstedt, 1913.

nn. [Swed.] *Skolan och samhället.* Trans. Walborg
Hedberg. [Extract] in *Andra bearbetade
upplagen*, by B. R. Hall, pp. 98-105.
Stockholm: P. A. Norstedt, 1920.

oo. [Swed.] *Skolan och samhället.* Trans. Walborg
Hedberg. [Extract] in *Tredje bearbetade
upplagen*, by B. R. Hall, pp. 86-91.
Stockholm: P. A. Norstedt, 1925.

pp. [Swed.] *Skolan och samhället.* Trans. Walborg
Hedberg. [Extract] in *Fjärde bearbetade
och utvidgade upplagen*, by B. R. Hall,
pp. 93-98. Stockholm: P. A. Norstedt,
1949.

54. THE SCHOOL AND THE CHILD: Being Selections from
the Educational Essays of John Dewey
Ed. Joseph J. Findlay. London:
Blackie and Son Limited, [1907? Pref.
1906]. 128 pp.
[Contents:
The Child and the Curriculum.
Eight essays from the *Elementary School
Record*:
"The Kindergarten."
"General Principles of Work,
Educationally Considered."
"Historical Development of Inven-
tions and Occupations."
"Children of Eight Years of Age."
"Psychology of Occupations."
"Reflective Attention."
"The Aim of History in Elementary
Education."
"The Psychology of the Elementary
Curriculum."]

a. [Russ.] *Shkola i rebĕnok.* Trans. L. Azarevich.
Moscow: Gosizdat, 1922. 60 pp.
2nd printing, (Leningrad)
1923. 66 pp.

b. [Span.] *La escuela y el niño.* Trans. [with an
introd. by] Domingo Barnés. (Ciencia
y Educación, Sección Contemporánea,
Obras de Dewey, I) Madrid: La Lectura,
1926. 170 pp.
2nd printing, 1934. 166 pp.
3rd printing, 1936
[Contents:
"Ensayo sobre el curso de la escuela
elemental."
"Los principios generales del trabajo
educativamente considerados."
"Desenvolvimiento histórico de los
inventos y ocupaciones."
"Introducción general."
"Psicología de las ocupaciones."
"Atención reflexiva."
"La finalidad de la historia en la
instrucción primaria."
"La psicología del programa
elemental."]

55. SCHOOLS OF TOMORROW
    (with Evelyn Dewey). New York: E. P. Dutton and
    Co., [c1915]. 316 pp.

a. [Arab.] *Madāris al-mustaqbal*. Trans. 'Abd al-
            Fattāḥ al-Minyāwī. Cairo: Maktabat
            al-Nahḍah al-Miṣrīyah, 1965. 344 pp.

b. [Bulg.] *Bădăsteto učilište*. Trans. T. Samodumov.
            (Biblioteka Nauka i Văzpitanie, I)
            Sofia: Nauka i Văzpitanie, 1924.
            156 pp.

c. [Chin.] *Ming-jih chih hsüeh-hsiao*. Trans.
            Ching-nung Chu and Tzu-nien P'an.
            Shanghai: The Commercial Press, 1923.
            286 pp.
                        2nd printing, 1935

d. [Fren.] *Les écoles de demain*. Trans. R. Duthil.
            (Education) Paris: Flammarion, 1931.
            284 pp.

e. [Jap.] *Kyōiku kyōju no kaizō*. Trans. Sajū
           Tasei. Tokyo: Kodōkan, 1920. 494 pp.

f. [Jap.] *Asu no gakkō*. Trans. Tokuji Yamashita.
           Tokyo: Kōseikaku, 1939. 432 pp.

g. [Rum.] *Şcoalele de mâine*. Trans. G. I. Simion.
           Bucharest: Editura Librăriei Principele
           Mircea, 1937. xix, 263 pp.

h. [Russ.] *Shkoly budushchego*. Trans. R. Landsberg
            [pref. by I. I. Gorbunov-Posadov].
            (Biblioteka Svobodnogo Vospitaniya i
            Obrazovaniya i Zashchity Detei, CXIII)
            Moscow: [n.p.], 1918. 104 pp.

i. [Russ.] *Shkoly budushchego*. Trans. R. Landsberg
            [with an introd. by I. I. Gorbunov-
            Posadov]. Berlin: State Publishing
            House of the R.S.F.S.R., 1922. 179 pp.

j. [Russ.] *Shkoly budushchego*. Trans. R. Landsberg
            [with an introd. by Lebedev-Polianskii].
            Moscow: Rabotnik Prosveshcheniya, 1922.
            152 pp.
                        2nd printing, 1922. 196 pp.

k. [Span.] *Las escuelas de mañana.* Trans. Lorenzo
Luzuriaga. Madrid: Hernando, 1918.
311 pp.
> 2nd printing, [Corrected]
> 1927. 320 pp.
> 3rd printing, 1930. 311 pp.

l. [Span.] *Las escuelas de mañana.* Trans. Lorenzo
Luzuriaga. Buenos Aires: Losada, 1950.
177 pp.
> 2nd printing, 1957
> 3rd printing, 1961. 184 pp.

m. [Swed.] *Framtidsskolor.* Trans. N. G. W. Lager-
stedt. (Padagogiska Skrifter Utgivna av
Sverges Allmänna Folkskollärareförenings
Litteratursällskap, LXXXII-LXXXIII)
Lund: Lindstedts Universitetsbokhandel,
1917-18. 228 pp.

n. [Turk.] *Yarinin mektepleri.* Trans. S. Celâl
Antel. Istanbul: Kanaat Kitabevi,
1938. 265 pp.

Schools of Tomorrow [Selection(s)]

o. [Bulg.] "Svoboda i individualnost" ("Freedom and
Individuality"). [Trans.?] In *Svobodno
vǎzpitanie,* II, 9-10 (1923-24), 273-80.

p. [Bulg.] *Obrazovanie črez trud (Education through
Industry).* [Trans.?] (Biblioteka Dom i
Učilište, I) Sofia: Hudožnik, 1935.
32 pp.

q. [Czech] "Výchova k práci" ("Education through
Industry"). Trans. A. A. Hoch. In
Osobnost a práce, by V. M. Bechterev,
pp. 37-58. Prague: J. Pelcl, 1922.

56. "The Social-Economic Situation and Education,"
(with John L. Childs). William Heard Kilpatrick,
ed., pp. 32-72. New York, London: The
Century Co., [c1933].

a. [Span.] "La situación económico-social y la
educación." [Trans.?] In *Anales de*

instrucción primaria, [Montevideo, Uruguay], II, XIV, 5, 6, 7 (May-July 1951), 155-66.

57. "Some Factors in Mutual National Understanding," *Kaizō* (Tokyo), III, 3 (Mar. 1921), 17-28.

   a. [Jap.]   "Tōyō bummei wa seishinteki ni shite seiyō bummei wa busshiteki nari ya" ("Is Eastern Culture Spiritual and Western Culture Materialistic?"). [Trans.?] In *Kaizō*, III, 3 (Mar. 1921), 103-14.

58. THE SOURCES OF A SCIENCE OF EDUCATION
New York: Horace Liveright, 1929. 77 pp.

   a. [Chin.]   *Chiao-yü k'o-hsüeh chih ch'üan-yüan.* Trans. Tai-nien Chang. [n.p.]: Jen-Wen Bookstore, [n.d.]. [pp.?]

   b. [Chin.]   *Chiao-yü k'o-hsüeh chih tzu-yüan.* Trans. Chin-chang Ch'iu. Shanghai: The Commercial Press, 1936. [pp.?]

   c. [Czech]   *O pramenech vysokoškolské vědy.* Trans. J. Gvardián. Prague: Samcovo Knihkupectví, 1947. 116 pp.

   d. [Germ.]   "Die Quellen einer Wissenschaft von der Erziehung," in *Der Projekt-Plan*, pp. 102-41. [*See 67*]

   e. [Hebr.]   "Ha-mekorot lemada ha-hinukh." Trans. A. Z. Brawn [ed. H. Ilan]. In *Nissayon ve-hinukh*, [pp.?]. Jerusalem: The School for Education of the Hebrew University and the Ministry of Culture and Education, 1960. [*See 14k*]

   f. [Ital.]   *Le fonti di una scienza dell'educazione.* Trans. Mariuma Tioli-Gabrieli. (Educatori Antichi e Moderni, LXXVI) Florence: La Nuova Italia, 1951. viii, 58 pp.

g. [Jap.]   *Kyōiku kagaku no hongen.* Trans. Hiroshi
           Sugiura. Tokyo: Meigen Shobō, 1966.
           154 pp.

h. [Span.] "La ciencia de la educación." Trans.
           Lorenzo Luzuriaga. In *La ciencia de la
           educación* [Pt. I], pp. 1-80. (Biblio-
           teca del Maestro, VI) Buenos Aires:
           Losada, 1941. [Includes *9a*]
                        2nd printing, 1944
                        3rd printing, 1948
                        4th printing, 1951
                        5th printing, 1957
                        6th printing, 1960
                        7th printing, 1964

59. "Spencer and Bergson," *Revue de métaphysique et
     de morale,* LXX, 3 (July-Sept. 1965), 327-30.

  a. [Fren.] "Spencer et Bergson." Trans. Gérard
             Deledalle. In *Revue de métaphysique et
             de morale,* LXX, 3 (July-Sept. 1965),
             330-33.

60. THEORY OF VALUATION
     (International Encyclopedia of Unified Science,
                Vol. II. Foundations of the Unity of
                Science, No. 4) Chicago: University
                of Chicago Press, [c1939]. 67 pp.

  a. [Ital.] *Teoria della valutazione.* Trans. For-
             tunato Brancatisano [with an introd. by
             Aldo Visalberghi]. (Pensatori Antichi
             e Moderni, LVI) Florence: La Nuova
             Italia, 1960. xxx, 104 pp.

  b. [Jap.] *Hyōka no riron.* Trans. Tomohiko Isono.
            Kyoto: Bekishoin, 1957. 151 pp.

  c. [Span.] *Teoría de la evaluación.* Trans. and
             published by the Facultad de Filosofía
             y Letras de Buenos Aires, 1958. 26 pp.

61. "Unity of Science as a Social Problem," in
    International Encyclopedia of Unified Science.
    Eds. Otto Neurath, *et al*., pp. 29-38.
    Chicago: University of Chicago Press,
    [c1938].

   a. [Ital.] "Unità della scienza come problèma
    sociale." Trans. Orio Peduzzi. In
    Neopositivismo e unità della scienza,
    pp. 55-69. Milan: Bompiani, 1958.

62. THE WAY OUT OF EDUCATIONAL CONFUSION
    Cambridge: Harvard University Press, 1931.
    41 pp.

   a. [Germ.] "Der Ausweg aus dem pädagogischen Wirr-
    warr," in *Der Projekt-Plan*, pp. 85-101.
    [*See 67*]

63. "What I Believe," *Forum*, LXXXIII (Mar. 1930),
    176-82.

   a. [Arab.] [Title?] Trans. Ahmad Fu'ād al-Ahwānī.
    In *John Dewey*, by Ahmad Fu'ād al-Ahwānī,
    [pp.?]. Cairo: Dār al-Ma'ārif 1959.

   b. [Bulg.] "Moeto kredo." Trans. "A. C." In
    Svobodno văzpitanie, XIV, 5-6 (1935-36),
    178-82.

   c. [Swed.] "Tro och erfarenhet" ("Belief and Ex-
    perience"). Trans. [with a foreword by]
    Alf Ahlberg. In *Min Tro; ein bok om
    livråskådningar*, pp. 121-42. Stockholm:
    Natur och Kultur, 1941.

64. L'ECOLE ET L'ENFANT
    Trans. L. S. Pidoux [with an introd. by Edouard
    Claparède]. (Collection d'Actualités
    Pédagogiques) Neuchâtel: Delachaux &
    Niestlé, S. A., 1913. xxxii, 136 pp.

2nd printing, 1922
3rd printing, 1931
4th printing, 1947. 174 pp.
  (Actualités Pédagogiques
  et Psychologiques)
5th printing, 1953
6th printing, 1962

[Contents:
"Interest as Related to [the Training
  of the] Will" (27).
The Child and the Curriculum (4).
"The Aim of History in Elementary Edu-
  cation" (1).
"Ethical Principles Underlying Educa-
  tion" (18).]

a. [Bulg.] *Učilišteto i deteto*. Trans. Efr. Beldedov. (Biblioteka Pedagogičeski, II)
Sofia: Herman Pole, 1934. 108 pp.

b. [Ital.] *Saggi pedagogici*. Trans. [with an
introd. by] Maria Teresa Gentile.
Florence: Vallecchi Editore, S.p.A.,
1950. xlvi, 102 pp.

c. [Kor.] *Hakkyo wa adong*. Trans. Chŏngŭmsa.
Seoul: Chŏngŭmsa, 1947. 117 pp.
[This title translates "School and
Children"; therefore, it may be a trans-
lation of *The School and the Child*,
(54).]

d. [Pol.] *Szkoła i dziecko*. Trans. Helena Bles-
zyńska. Warsaw: E. Wende, 1923.
165 pp.

e. [Pol.] *Szkoła i dziecko*. Trans. Helena Bles-
zyńska. Warsaw: Biblioteka Dziel
Naukowych, 1929. 165 pp.
          2nd printing, 1930
          3rd printing, 1933

f. [Rum.] *Şcoala şi copilul*. Trans. I. G. Marin-
escu. Bucharest: Cîmpulung, 1914.
116 pp.

g. [Rum.] *Şcoala şi copilul*. Trans. I. G. Marin-
escu [corrected and rev.]. Bucharest:

Editura H. Steinberg și Fiul, 1923.
147 pp.

65. ENSAYOS DE EDUCACION
Trans. Domingo Barnés. (Ciencia y Educación,
Sección Contemporánea, Obras de Dewey,
II) Madrid: La Lectura, 1926.
174 pp.
[Contents:
"Ethical Principles Underlying Educa-
tion" (*12*).
"Interest as Related to [the Training
of the] Will" (*27*).
Democracy and Education (Selection:
"Interest and Discipline") (*8*).
"My Pedagogic Creed" (*36*).
"Psychology and Social Practice" (*47*).]

66. IL MIO CREDO PEDAGOGICO: ANTOLOGIA DEI SCRITTI
SULL'EDUCAZIONE
Trans. Enzo Enriques Agnoletti, Lamberto
Borghi, Ernesto Codignola. Ed. [with an
introd. by] Lamberto Borghi. (Educatori
Antichi e Moderni, CXXXVI) Florence:
La Nuova Italia, (Feb.) 1954.
liv, 270 pp.
2nd printing, (Dec.) 1954
3rd printing, 1959
4th printing, 1961
5th printing, 1963
6th printing, 1965
7th printing, 1966

[Contents:
"My Pedagogic Creed" (*36*), from *11b*.
Democracy and Education (*8*), Chs. X,
XI, XII from *8j*.
"Democracy and Educational Administra-
tion" (*11d*), Ch. 43 from *11b*.
"Democracy and Education in the World
of Today" (*11e*), Ch. 45 from *11b*.
Experience and Education (*14*), Chs.
III, IV, V, VII from *14l*.
The School and Society (*53*), Chs. I,
II, IV from *53m*.]

67. DER PROJEKT-PLAN: GRUNDLEGUNG UND PRAXIS
Trans. Georg Schultz and Ernst Wiesenthal.
(Pädagogik des Auslands herausgegeben
im Auftrag des Zentralinstituts für
Erziehung und Unterricht von Prof.
Dr. Peter Petersen, Jena, VI) Weimar:
Herman Böhlaus Nachfolger, 1935.
213 pp.
[Contents (Dewey only):
The Way Out of Educational Confusion
(62).
The Sources of a Science of Education
(58).
The Child and the Curriculum (4).
"How Much Freedom in New Schools?"
(19).]

II Writings Translated into English,

First Published in Another Language

68. "Le développement du pragmatisme américain."
[Trans.?] In *Revue de métaphysique et de morale*, XXIX (Oct. 1922), 411-40.

   a. [Eng.] "The Development of American Pragmatism." Trans. Herbert W. Schneider. In *Studies in the History of Ideas* (by the Department of Philosophy of Columbia University), II. New York: Columbia University Press, 1925. Supplement, pp. 353-77.

69. "L'éducation au point de vue social." [Trans.?] In *L'année pédagogique*, III (1913), 32-48.

   a. [Eng.] "Education from a Social Viewpoint." Trans. Jo Ann Boydston. In *Educational Theory*, XV, 2 (Apr. 1965), 73-84.

70. "Preface" [English ed.] in *La terreur à Cuba*. Paris: Courbevoie, la Cootypographie, 1933. Pp. 9-10.

   a. [Eng.] "Terror in Cuba in 1933." Trans. Jo Ann Boydston. In *School and Society*, 96 (23 Nov. 1968), pp. 444-45.

71. "Trois facteurs indépendants en matière de morale." Trans. Charles Cestre. In *Bulletin de la société française de philosophie*, XXX (Oct.-Dec. 1930), 118-27. [Discussion, pp. 127-35.]

   a. [Eng.] "Three Independent Factors in Morals." Trans. Jo Ann Boydston. In *Educational Theory*, XVI, 3 (July 1966), 197-209.

III Published Writings Not Translated into English

72. ["Idealism in Natural Science"] "Shizen kagaku ni okeru risōshugi." [Trans.?] In *Kaizō*, III, 4 (Apr. 1921), 198-208.

73. ["The Pacific Conference"] "Taiheiyō kaigi." [Trans.?] In *Kaizō*, III, 9 (Sept. 1921), 235-40.

74. ["A Philosophical Interpretation of Human Prejudice"] "Jinshuteki henken no tetsugakuteki kaishaku." [Trans.?] In *Kaizō*, III, 8 (Aug. 1921), 73-90.

75. ["Science and the Present Industrial System"] "Kagaku to genkon no sangyō seido." [Trans.?] In *Kaizō*, III, 5 (May 1921), 198-208.

[English translations of titles made by Victor Kobayashi.]

IV Published Lectures Not

Translated into English

AN ALPHABETICAL LISTING OF BOOKS, PERIODICALS,
AND NEWSPAPERS IN WHICH THE CHINESE LECTURES
WERE PUBLISHED

Academic Lamp (Hsüeh teng). A supplement to *The China Times*.

Awakening (Chüeh-wu). A supplement to *Republic Daily*.

Bulletin of the Ministry of Education (Chiao-yü pu kung-pao). An official monthly journal published in Peking.

The China Times (Shih-shih hsin-pao). A Shanghai daily newspaper.

Citizens' Gazette (Kuo-min kung-pao). A Peking daily newspaper, closed by the government in the fall of 1920.

Collected Speeches of Dewey and Russell (Tu-wei Lo-su yen-chiang lu ho-k'an). [Interpreter, recorder?] Shanghai: T'ai-tung t'u-shu-kuan, 1921. iv, 112 pp., (Dewey), 1i, 52 pp., (Russell).

Democracy and Education (P'ing-min chiao-yü). A periodical published weekly in Peking in 1919, fortnightly from Nov. 1920.

Democracy and Education (P'ing-min chu-i yü chiao-yü). Recorded and translated by Tao-chih Ch'ang. Shanghai: The Commercial Press, 1922. 368 pp. Based on class notes taken from Dewey's lectures at Peking Teachers' College. The translator advises that the notes should be used as an explanatory guide to the work *Democracy and Education*.

Dewey's Lectures in Fukien (Tu-wei Fu-chien chiang-yen lu). Fukien: Board of Education, 1920, [pp.?]. Contains lectures delivered in Fukien province.

The Eastern Miscellany (Tung-fang tsa-chih). A fortnightly periodical published in Shanghai.

The Educational Philosophy of Dewey (Tu-wei chiao-yü che-hsüeh). Recorded by Hai-kuan Chin. Shanghai: The Commercial Press, 1922. 111 pp. One version of lectures delivered at Nanking Teachers' College.

Educational Tide (Chiao-yü ch'ao). A monthly periodical published in Hangchow, Chekiang province.

Five Major Lectures of Dewey (Tu-wei wu ta chiang-yen). Peking: Morning Post, 1920. [Interpreter Shih Hu; recorders Fu-yüan Sun, Wang Wu, Ch'un Ch'iu, Shao-yü Kuo.

The Magazine of the Kwangtung Education Association (Kuang-tung sheng chiao-yü hui tsa-chih). A monthly periodical published in Canton.

Morning Post (Ch'en pao). A daily newspaper published in Peking.

Morning Post Supplement (Ch'en pao fu-k'an). A daily supplement to the *Morning Post*.

The New China (Hsin Chung-kuo). A monthly periodical published in Peking.

The New Education (Hsin chiao-yü). A monthly periodical published in Peking.

New Kansu (Hsin lung). A monthly periodical published in Peking.

The New Tide (Hsin ch'ao). A monthly periodical published in Peking.

New Youth (Hsin ch'ing-nien). A monthly periodical published in Peking.

Republic Daily (Min-kuo jih-pao). A Shanghai daily newspaper.

Specimens of Paihua Style (Pen-hua wen-fan). 4 vols. Shanghai: The Commercial Press, 1920.

Three Major Lectures of Dewey (Tu-wei san ta yen-chiang). Interpreter Po-ming Liu; recorder Chen-sheng Shen. Shanghai: T'ai-tung T'u-shu-kuan, 1920. Three series, 80 pp., 71 pp., 69 pp.

Weekly Critic (Mei-chou p'ing-lun). A weekly periodical published in Peking, suppressed in Aug. 1919.

The Youth and Society (Shao-nien she-hui). A weekly periodical published in Nanking.

76. "The Aim(s?) of Educational Administration" ("Chiao-
    yü hsing-cheng chih mu-ti"). Interpreter Hsiao-
    ts'ang Cheng, [recorder?].
        Awakening, 9 July 1920.

77. "The Aims of Science Education" ("Li-k'o chiao-
    yü chih mu-ti"). Trans. Ch'i Chiang. [Transla-
    tion of a speech delivered at Tokyo Imperial
    University, Japan.]
        The New Education, I, 5 (Aug. 1919), 480-85.

78. "Citizenship Education" ("Kung-min chiao-yü").
    [Interpreter and recorder?] [Delivered at P'u-
    tung High School near Shanghai.]
        Awakening, 4 June 1920.
        Collected Speeches of Dewey and Russell,
            pp. 63-68.

79. "The Concept of 'Right' in Western Thought"
    ("Hsi-fang ssu-hsiang chung chih ch'üan-li kuan-
    nien"). Interpreter Shih Hu, recorders T'ung-
    chao Wang and Ping Hsieh. [Delivered at the
    Chinese University in Peking.]
        Academic Lamp, 27, 28 Jan. 1920.
        Awakening, 27 Jan. 1920.
        Bulletin of the Ministry of Education,
            Mar. 1920, 39-43.

80. "Criteria for Social Progress" ("She-hui chin-
    hua chih piao-chun"). Interpreter Po-ming Liu,
    recorder I. Ch'iu.
        Academic Lamp, 11 May 1920.

81. "Cultivation of Character as the Ultimate Aim of
    Education" ("P'in-ke chih yang-ch'eng wei chiao-
    yü chih wu shang mu-ti"). Interpreter Shih Hu,
    recorder Ch'u-min Teng. [Delivered at Shansi
    University, with *139*.]
        The New China, I, 7 (15 Nov. 1919), 55-58.
        Bulletin of the Ministry of Education,
            Nov. 1919, 47-49. [Final two paragraphs
            missing.]
        Collected Speeches of Dewey and Russell,
            pp. 86-91.

82. "Democracy and Education" ("P'ing-min chu-i yü
    chiao-yü"). Recorders Chi-min Li and Wen-mien
    Yang. [Classroom lectures by Dewey using

Democracy and Education as a text, delivered at
Peking Teachers' College.]

    Academic Lamp, 5, 10, 12, 17-19 Nov. 1920.
      [Lectures 1-6.]
    Democracy and Education. Recorder and
      translator Tao-chih Ch'ang. XXVI (20 Dec.
      1920)-XLII (10 Nov. 1921), *passim*.
    Democracy and Education. Recorder and trans-
      lator Tao-chih Ch'ang. 368 pp. [The trans-
      lator took notes in English, elaborated them
      in Chinese, and advises readers that it
      should be used as an explanatory guide to
      Dewey's *Democracy and Education (8)*.]

83. "The Development of Democracy in America" ("Mei-
kuo chih min-chih ti fa-chan"). Interpreter
Shih Hu, recorders first and second lecture I-han
Kao, third lecture Shih Hu. [Three lectures delivered in Peking.]
    Weekly Critic, 26 (15 June 1919), 1-4.
    Morning Post Supplement, 17-20 June 1919.
    Awakening, 20-30 June 1919.
    Academic Lamp, 21, 23, 27, 28 June 1919.
    The New China, I, 3 (15 July 1919), 83-95.
    Bulletin of the Ministry of Education,
      Aug. 1919, 1-15.

84. "The Duty of Educators" ("Chiao-yü-chia chih
t'ien-chih"). Interpreter Po-ming Liu, recorder
I. Ch'iu. [Dewey delivered lectures on this
topic several times during May-June 1920 in the
Shanghai-Nanking area.]
    Academic Lamp, 14 May 1920.

85. "The Duty of Educators" ("Chiao-yü-che ti t'ien-
chih"). [Same topic, but different text than *84*.
Delivered on the 15th anniversary of the Second
Teachers' College (Shanghai?).]
    Awakening, 30 May 1920. [Interpreter and
      recorder?]
    Academic Lamp, 31 May 1920. Interpreter
      Po-ming Liu, recorder "a student."

86. "Education and Industry" ("Chiao-yü yü shih-yeh").
[This lecture is probably different from both *87*
and *109*.]
    Awakening, 2 July 1920. [Interpreter and
      recorder?]

Academic Lamp, 9 July 1920. Interpreter
Hsiao-ts'ang Cheng, recorders Tan Ch'en
and Ping-k'uei Shen.

87. "Education and Industry" ("Chiao-yü yü shih-yeh").
[Interpreter and recorder?] [Delivered at the
Y.M.C.A. in Foochow, Fukien province.]
Morning Post Supplement, 13, 14 May 1921.
Bulletin of the Ministry of Education,
Dec. 1921, 25-28.

88. ["Education for Interaction."] [English title
derived from the content by Dr. Robert Clopton.]
[Interpreter and recorder?] [Second Canton lecture delivered at the Kwangtung Provincial Education Association.]
*The Magazine of the Kwangtung Education
Association*, I, 1 (July 1921), 120-22.

89. "Educational Factors" ("Chiao-yü chih yao-su").
Interpreter Po-ming Liu, recorder I. Ch'iu.
Academic Lamp, 12 May 1920.

90. "Educators as Leaders in Society" ("Chiao-yü che
wei she-hui ling-shou"). [Interpreter and
recorder?] [Delivered at the First Teachers'
College of Fukien province.]
Morning Post Supplement, 30 Apr.-2 May 1921.
Bulletin of the Ministry of Education,
Aug. 1921, 33-35.

91. "The Essential Meaning of Vocational Education"
("Chih-yeh chiao-yü ti ching-i"). [Interpreter
and recorder?] [Delivered at the Vocational
Education Association (Shanghai?).]
Awakening, 31 May 1920.

92. "Essentials of Democratic Politics" ("Min-pen
cheng-chih chih chi-pen"). [Interpreter and
recorder?] [Delivered at the Private Fukien
College of Law and Administration.]
Bulletin of Ministry of Education, Sept.
1921, 40-42.

93. "Experimentalism" ("Shih-yen chu-i"). [Inter-
preter and recorder?] [Delivered at Wusih,
Kiangsu province.]
Awakening, 16 July 1920.

94. "Experimental Logic" ("Shih-yen lun-li hsüeh").
    [Approximately eighteen lectures delivered at
    Nanking Teachers' College.]
    > *Awakening*, 10-12 July 1919. Interpreter
    > and recorder Po-ming Liu.
    > *Academic Lamp*, 19 Apr.-19 June 1920, *passim*.
    > Interpreter Po-ming Liu, recorders Ch'eng-
    > feng Hsia and Ch'u Ts'ao.
    > *Morning Post Supplement*, 20 Sept.-20 Oct.
    > 1920, *passim*. Interpreter and recorder
    > Po-ming Liu.
    > *Bulletin of the Ministry of Education*,
    > Nov. 1920-Feb. 1921, *passim*. Inter-
    > preter Po-ming Liu, recorders Ch'eng-
    > feng Hsia and Ch'u Ts'ao.
    > *Three Major Lectures of Dewey*. Inter-
    > preter Po-ming Liu, recorder Chen-
    > sheng Shen. 69 pp. [Pt. III, appar-
    > ently ten lectures.]

95. "Factors Creating Motivation in Education"
    ("Tsao chiu fa-tung ti hsing-chih ti chiao-yü").
    [Interpreter and recorder?]   [Delivered at the
    First Teachers' College, Hangchow.]
    > *Awakening*, 17 June 1920.

96. "Habit and Thought" ("Hsi-kuan yü ssu-hsiang").
    [Interpreter and recorder?] [Delivered at the
    Y.M.C.A. in Foochow, Fukien province.]
    > *Morning Post Supplement*, 30 June-1 July 1921.
    > *Bulletin of the Ministry of Education*,
    > Oct. 1921, 39-41.

97. "History of Philosophy" ("Che-hsüeh shih").
    [Approximately nineteen lectures, limited to
    Greek philosophy, delivered at Nanking Teachers'
    College.]
    > *Morning Post Supplement*, 9 Apr.-29 June
    > 1920, *passim*. Interpreter Po-ming Liu,
    > recorder Fan Che.
    > *Academic Lamp*, 16 Apr.-24 June 1920,
    > *passim*. [Ten lectures.] Interpreter
    > Po-ming Liu, recorders Fan Chung, Shuang-
    > chiu Shao, and Yü-lin Shih.
    > *Bulletin of the Ministry of Education*,
    > Aug. 1920, 39-45; Sept. 1920, 25-34;
    > Oct. 1920, 35-42. Interpreter [first
    > six parts] Po-ming Liu, recorder Fan
    > Chung.

Three Major Lectures of Dewey. Interpreter Po-ming Liu, recorder Chen-
shang Shen.   79 pp·

98. "The Importance of Dynamic Morality" ("Tung-tso
tao-te chung-yao ti yüan-yin"). [Interpreter
and recorder?] [First Canton lecture delivered
at the Higher Normal School.]
      *The Magazine of the Kwangtung Education
      Association,* I, 1 (July 1921), 116-19.

99. "Impressions from Travelling in the South" ("Nan-
yu hsin-ying"). [Interpreter?], recorder Lan
Shu.
      Morning Post Supplement, 17-19 June 1921.
      Awakening, 22 June 1921. [Recorder?]
      Academic Lamp, 3 July 1921.
      Bulletin of the Ministry of Education,
         Oct. 1921, 29-33.
      Collected Speeches of Dewey and Russell,
         pp. 103-11.

100. "Independent Action and Self-Government" ("Tse-
tung yü tsu-chih"). [Interpreter and recorder?]
[Delivered at the First High School of Fukien
province.]
      Morning Post Supplement, 3-6 May 1921.
      Bulletin of the Ministry of Education,
         July 1921, 41-44.

101. "The Meaning of a University" ("Ta-hsüeh ti chih-
ch'u"). [Interpreter and recorder?]
      Morning Post Supplement, 25, 26 Apr. 1921.

102. "The Meaning of Democracy" ("Min-chih ti i-i").
[Interpreter and recorder?] [Delivered at the
Fukien Shang-yu Club.]
      Morning Post Supplement, 8 July 1921.
      Bulletin of the Ministry of Education,
         Sept. 1921, 54-55.

103. "Methods for Measuring Intelligence--in Outline"
("Chih-hui tu-liang-fa ti ta-kang").
      Academic Lamp, 26 May 1920. [Interpreter?],
         recorder Lang San.
      Awakening, 27 May 1920. [Interpreter and
         recorder?]

104. [Nanking Lectures.] [Transliterated title?]
     Interpreter Chih-hsing T'ao, *et al.*, [recorder?].
     [Lectures delivered 18, 19, 21, 24-26 May 1919
     at Nanking Teachers' College.]
         [Publication?]

105. "The New Conception of Life" ("Hsin jen-sheng-
     kuan").
         Academic Lamp, 18 Apr. 1920. Interpreter
           Po-ming Liu, recorder Ch'u Ts'ao.
         Academic Lamp, 4 June 1920. Interpreter
           Po-ming Liu, recorder Kung-chan P'an.
           [Different text than above.]
         The Youth and Society, II, 3 (1 May 1920),
           [pp.? Incomplete text.] Interpreter
           Po-ming Liu, recorder Wen-chou Ni.
         Awakening, 3 June 1920. [Interpreter and
           recorder?]

106. "New Problems of Knowledge" ("Hsüeh-wen ti hsin
     wen-t'i"). Interpreter Shih Hu, recorders Hsi
     Chih and Wang Wu. [Delivered at the New Learning
     Association in Peking.]
         Awakening, 14, 15, 21, 22 Aug. 1919.
           [Interpreter and recorder?]
         Academic Lamp, 15 Aug. 1919.
         The New China, I, 5 (15 Sept. 1919), 236-40.
         The Eastern Miscellany, XVI, 9 (Sept. 1919),
           205-9.
         Educational Tide, I, 4 (Sept. 1919), [pp.?]
         Bulletin of the Ministry of Education,
           Sept. 1919, 19-24.

107. "New Trends in Education and the Reorganization
     of Teaching Methods" ("Chiao-yü ti hsin ch'u-
     shih yü chiao-ts'ai kai-tsu"). [Delivered in
     Soochow, Kiangsu province.]
         Academic Lamp, 23 June 1920. Inter-
           preter Po-ming Liu, recorder Tsu-
           shan Shen.
         Awakening, 24 June 1920. [Interpreter
           and recorder?]

108. "New Trends in Teaching Mathematics" ("Shu-yü ti
     hsin ch'u-shih"). [Interpreter and recorder?]
         Awakening, 30 June 1920.

109. "On Industrial Education" ("Shih-yeh chiao-yü
     lun"). [Interpreter and recorder?]

The New China, I, 5 (15 Sept. 1919),
234-36.
The Eastern Miscellany, XVI, 9 (Sept.
1919), 223-24.

110. "On the Chinese Fine Arts" ("Lun Chung-kuo ti
mei-shu"). Interpreter Shih Hu, recorders
P'ei-yen Ts'ao and Hui-po Wang. [Delivered to
the Fine Arts Club of Peking Teachers' College.]
Morning Post Supplement, 7 Mar. 1921.
Academic Lamp, 15 Mar. 1921.
Bulletin of the Ministry of Education,
Apr. 1921, 47-49.

111. "The Organization of American Education Associa-
tions and their Influence on Society" ("Mei-kuo
chiao-yü hui chih tsu-chih chi ch'i ying-hsiang
yü she-hui"). [Interpreter and recorder?]
[Delivered at Fukien Provincial Education Association (Foochow?).]
Morning Post Supplement, 7 May 1921.
Bulletin of the Ministry of Education,
Oct. 1921, 35-37.

112. "The Organization of Student Government" ("Hsüeh-
sheng tzu-chih ti tsu-chih").
Academic Lamp, 9 July 1920. Interpreter
Shen-wen Pan, recorders Tan Ch'en and
Ping-k'uei Shen.
Morning Post Supplement, 16-19 Sept.
1920. [Interpreter and recorder?]
Bulletin of the Ministry of Education,
Oct. 1920, 51-53. Interpreter Hsiao-
ts'ang Cheng.

113. "The Organization of Teaching Materials" ("Chiao-
ts'ai ti tsu-chih"). Interpreter Po-ming Liu,
recorders Meng-chiu Cheng and Tsai-tsu Hsü.
[Delivered in Soochow, Kiangsu province.]
Awakening, 1 July 1920.

114. "The Philosophy of Education" ("Chiao-yü che-
hsüeh"). Interpreter Shih Hu, recorder Fu-yüan
Sun. [A series of sixteen lectures delivered in
Peking.]
Academic Lamp, 25 Sept. 1919-7 Mar. 1920,
passim. [25, 26 Sept., recorder Wang Wu.]

Awakening, 28 Sept. 1919-6 Mar. 1920,
passim. [28 Sept.-1 Oct., recorder
Wang Wu.]
Bulletin of the Ministry of Education,
Oct. 1919-June 1920, *passim*.
The New China, I, 6 (15 Oct. 1919)-II,
7 (15 July 1920), *passim*.
Five Major Lectures of Dewey, pp. 127-258.
Morning Post Supplement, 26 Feb. 1920-
23 Aug. 1920, *passim*.

Translations:
a. [Jap.] [Title?] Trans. Yoshio Nagano. In *Dyūi
no kyōiku tetsugaku* by Yoshio Nagano.
Tokyo: Chūwa Shoin, 1949. [pp.?]
b. [Jap.] [Title?] Trans. Yoshio Nagano. In *Dyūi
"kyōiku tetsugaku" no "gendai sanko tetsugakka"* by Yoshio Nagano. Tokyo:
Shunjūsha, 1951. [pp.?]
2nd printing, 1952

115. "Philosophy of Education" ("Chiao-yü che-hsüeh").
Interpreter Po-ming Liu. [This is one version
of a series of 20-30 lectures delivered at
Nanking Teachers' College, which differs from
two other series also delivered on the philosophy of education in Peking.]
Academic Lamp, 13, 15, 17, 20, 21 Apr.
1920. Parts 1-5, recorder Hai-kuan Chin.
24, 26 Apr. 1920. Parts 6, 7, recorders
Chih-fang Kuo and Hai-kuan Chin.
10 May 1920. Part 8(?), recorder Chih-
mien Shih.
11, 14 May 1920. Parts 9, 11, recorders
Nien-tsu Chang and Chih-fang Kuo.
19, 23 May 1920. Parts 11, 12, recorders
Hai-kuan Chin and Wen-chou Ni.
30 May 1920. Part 14, recorders Chih-fang
Kuo and Hai-kuan Chin.
2, 7 July 1920. Parts 15, 19, recorders
Hai-kuan Chin and Wen-chou Ni.
3, 12 July 1920. Parts 16, 20, recorders
Wen-chou Ni and Nien-tsu Chang.
5, 6, 14 July 1920. Parts 17, 18, 21,
recorders Nien-tsu Chang and Chih-fang Kuo.
15 July 1920. Part 22, recorders Chih-fang
Kuo and Hai-kuan Chin.
Bulletin of the Ministry of Education, July
1920, 27-37. Recorder Hai-kuan Chin.

Aug. 1920, 35-40. Recorders Chih-fang Kuo
and Hai-kuan Chin.
Sept. 1920, 27-33. [Recorder(s)?].
Oct. 1920, 39-50. Recorders Wen-chou Ni
and Nien-tsu Chang.
Nov. 1920, 29-33. Recorders Chih-fang Kuo
and Nien-tsu Chang.
Dec. 1920, 43-48. Recorders Wen-chou Ni
and Nien-tsu Chang.
Three Major Lectures of Dewey. Recorder
Chen-sheng Shen. Part I, 151 pp.
The Educational Philosophy of Dewey. Record-
er Hai-kuan Chin. 111 pp.

116. "Present Opportunities in the Teaching Profes-
sion" ("Chiao-shih chih-yeh chih hsien-tsai chi-
hui"). Interpreter Cho-jan Wang. [Delivered at
the Peking Teachers' College. The text indicates
that this was probably Dewey's final public lec-
ture in Peking. The title "Farewell Address"
("Lin-peh tseng-yen") was given to this text in
Academic Lamp, 28 June 1921 and *Bulletin of the
Ministry of Education,* July 1921.]
Morning Post Supplement, 24-27 June 1921.
Recorder Lan Shu.
Awakening, 26, 27 June 1921. [Recorder?]
Academic Lamp, 28 June 1921. Recorder
Hsiao-chi Liu.
Academic Lamp, 3 July 1921. Recorder Lan
Shu.
Bulletin of the Ministry of Education,
July 1921, 47-51. [Recorder?]
Bulletin of the Ministry of Education,
Aug. 1921, 45-50. Recorder Lan Shu.
Collected Speeches of Dewey and Russell,
pp. 92-102.

117. "Principles of Training Youth in Education"
("Chiao-shou ch'ing-nien ti chiao-yü yüan-li").
[Interpreter?], recorder Yin Fu. [Delivered at
the Peking Women's Teachers' College.]
Morning Post Supplement, 10, 11 May 1921.
Bulletin of the Ministry of Education,
Aug. 1921, 51-53.

118. "The Problem of Social Progress" ("She-hui chin-
hua wen-t'i"). Interpreter Po-ming Liu, recorder Fan-chiu Fei.

Academic Lamp, 22 June 1920.

119. "Psychological Factors in Education ("Chiao-yü chih hsin-li ti yao-su"). [Interpreter and recorder?] [Fifth lecture delivered in the Tsinan series.]
   Morning Post Supplement, 19-21 Sept. 1921.
   Bulletin of the Ministry of Education, Nov. 1921, 15-20.

120. "The Question of Co-Education" ("Nan-nü t'ung-hsüeh wen-t'i"). [Interpreter and recorder?] [Delivered at the Kiangsu Provincial Education Association in Shanghai.]
   Awakening, 2 June 1920.
   Academic Lamp, 1 July 1920. Recorder Keng Hsiang.

121. "The Real Meaning of Democracy" ("Te-mo-k'e-la-hsi ti chen-i"). [Delivered in Hangchow.]
   Academic Lamp, 9 June 1920. Interpreter Po-ming Liu, recorder Hsiao-pai Li.
   Awakening, 16 June 1920. [Interpreter and recorder?]
   Specimens of Paihua Style. [Interpreter?], recorder Shih Hu. Vol. IV, pp. 87-94.

122. "The Real Meaning of Democratic Education" ("P'ing-min chiao-yü chih chen-ti"). Interpreter Tsung-hai Cheng, recorder Yü-k'uei Chu. [Delivered to the Chekiang Provincial Education Association in Hangchow.]
   Educational Tide, I, 2 (June 1919), 27-34.
   Awakening, 19-23 July 1919.

123. "The Real Meaning of Freedom" ("'Tzu-yu' ti chen-i"). [Interpreter and recorder?] [Delivered at Yangchow.]
   Awakening, 25 May 1920.

124. "The Real Meaning of Independent Action" ("Tzu-tung chih chen-i"). Interpreter Po-ming Liu, recorder Ch'ang-keng Ch'en.
   Academic Lamp, 29 May 1920.

125. "A Record of Dr. Dewey's Talk with the Education and Industry Observation Group from Kweichow Province" ("Tu-wei po-shih yü Kuei-chou chiao-yü

shih-yeh ts'an-kuan t'uan t'an-hua chi-lüeh").
[Interpreter and recorder?]
> *Academic Lamp*, 29 July 1919.
> *Awakening*, 27 Aug. 1919.

126. "A Record of Lectures on Ethics" ("Lun-li chiang-
yen chi-lüeh"). Interpreter Shih Hu, [recorder?].
[Fifteen lectures delivered in Peking.]
> *Morning Post Supplement*, 15 Oct. 1919-
> 1 Apr. 1920, *passim*.
> *Academic Lamp*, 18 Oct. 1919-5 Mar. 1920,
> *passim*. [Fourteen lectures.]
> *Bulletin of the Ministry of Education*,
> Nov. 1919-May 1920, *passim*.
> *The New China*, I, 7 (15 Nov. 1919)-II,
> 6 (15 June 1920), *passim*.
> *Awakening*, (lecture 11) 22 Jan. 1920;
> 12, 22 Mar. 1920; 4 Apr. 1920.
> *Five Major Lectures of Dewey*, pp. 399-
> 472. Recorder Ch'un Ch'iu.

Translations:
a. [Jap.] [Title?] Trans. Yoshio Nagano. In *Dyūi
no rinrigaku* by Yoshio Nagano. Tokyo:
Chūwa Shoin, 1947. [pp.?]
b. [Jap.] [Title?] Trans. Yoshio Nagano. In
Shinkō: Dyūi rinrigaku gaisetsu by
Yoshio Nagano. Tokyo: Shunjūsha, 1951.
[pp.?]

127. "The Relationship between Culture and Technology"
("Kung-i ho wen-hua ti kuan-hsi"). Interpreter
Po-ming Liu, recorder Nai-ch'ien Chao.
> *Academic Lamp*, 9 June 1920.

128. "The Relationship between Democracy and Education"
("P'ing-min chu-i, p'ing-min chu-i ti chiao-
yü, p'ing-min chiao-yü chu-i ti pan-fa"). Inter-
preter Monlin Chiang, recorder Kung-chan P'an.
[Two lectures delivered to the Kiangsu Provincial
Education Association in Shanghai.]
> *Academic Lamp*, 8, 9 May 1919.
> *Morning Post Supplement*, 9 May 1919.
> *Educational Tide*, I, 2 (June 1919), 85-93.
> *The New Education*, I, 3 (Apr. 1919),
> 326-33. [Actually published in May
> or later.]
> *Bulletin of the Ministry of Education*,
> Aug. 1919, 25-31.

Collected Speeches of Dewey and Russell,
   pp. 69-80.

129. "The Relationship between Education and Social
   Progress" ("Chiao-yü yü she-hui chin-hua ti kuan-
   hsi"). [Delivered in Yangchow.]
      Awakening, 23 May 1920. [Interpreter
         and recorder?]
      Academic Lamp, 25 May 1920. Interpreter
         Po-ming Liu, recorders Ch'ang-keng
         Ch'en and Ch'ang-nien Hsü.

130. "The Relationship between Education and Society"
   ("Chiao-yü yü she-hui ti kuan-hsi"). Interpreter
   Shou-wu Hsü, recorder Tseng-lien Li.
      Academic Lamp, 9 June 1920.

131. "The Relationship between Education and the
   State" ("Chiao-yü yü kuo-chia chih kuan-hsi").
   [Interpreter and recorder?] [Delivered at the
   Y.M.C.A. in Foochow, Fukien province.]
      Morning Post Supplement, 8, 9 May 1921.
      Bulletin of the Ministry of Education,
         Dec. 1921, 23-25.

132. "The Relationship between Elementary Education
   and the State" ("Kuo-min chiao-yü yü kuo-chia
   chih kuan-hsi"). [Interpreter?], recorder Hsuan
   Wei. [Delivered at the Y.M.C.A. in Foochow,
   Fukien province.]
      Morning Post Supplement, 20, 21 June 1921.
      Academic Lamp, 3 July 1921.
      Bulletin of the Ministry of Education,
         July 1921, 45-46.
      Collected Speeches of Dewey and Russell,
         pp. 111-12.

133. "The Relationship between Elementary Education
   and Vocational Education" ("P'u-t'ung chiao-yü
   yü chih-yeh chiao-yü chih kuan-hsi"). [Inter-
   preter and recorder?] [Delivered at Shanghai
   College.]
      Awakening, 5 June 1920.
      Academic Lamp, 5 June 1920. Recorder
         Shu-hua Feng.

134. "The Relationship of the Natural and Social En-
   vironments with Human Life" ("T'ien-jan huan-

ching she-hui huan-ching yü jen-sheng chih kuan-
hsi"). [Interpreter and recorder?] [Delivered
at the Y.M.C.A. in Foochow, Fukien province.]
Morning Post Supplement,/28, 29 June 1921.
Academic Lamp, 3 July 1921.
Bulletin of the Ministry of Education,
Aug. 1921, 42-45.
Collected Speeches of Dewey and Russell,
pp. 69-80.

135. "The Relationship of School and Society" ("Hsüeh-
hsiao yü she-hui ti kuan-hsi"). [Interpreter and
recorder?] [Sixth lecture in the Tsinan series.]
Morning Post Supplement, 22-24 Sept. 1921.
Bulletin of the Ministry of Education,
Feb. 1922, 13-16.

136. "The Responsibility of Educators" ("Chiao-yü-che
ti tse-jen"). [Delivered in Nantung, Kiangsu
province.]
Academic Lamp, 17, 18 June 1920. Interpreter Po-ming Liu, recorder Hung-hsüan
Lo.
Awakening, 19 June 1920. [Interpreter
and recorder?]

137. "The Responsibility of Educators" ("Chiao-yü-che
ti tse-jen"). Interpreter Hsiao-ts'ang Cheng.
[Delivered in Soochow, Kiangsu province.]
Awakening, 3 July 1920. Recorder Shih-
chou Chiang.
Academic Lamp, 9 July 1920. Recorders
Tan Ch'en and Ping-k'uei Shen.

138. "School and Society" ("Hsüeh-hsiao yü she-hui").
Academic Lamp, 9 July 1920. Interpreter
Hsiao-ts'ang Cheng, recorder Tan Ch'en
and Ping-k'uei Shen.
Awakening, 11 July 1920. [Interpreter
and recorder?]

139. "The School and the Village" ("Hsüeh-hsiao yü
hsiang-li"). Interpreter Shih Hu, recorder Ch'u-
min Teng. [Delivered to normal school students
in Shansi province.]
The New China, I, 7 (15 Nov. 1919), 58-62.

140. ["The Scientific Spirit and Morality."] [English
title derived from the content by Dr. Robert

Clopton.] [Interpreter and recorder?] [Third
Canton lecture delivered at the Kwangtung
Provincial Education Association.]
 *The Magazine of the Kwangtung Education
  Association*, I, 1 (July 1921), 123-26.

141. "Social and Political Philosophy" ("She-huei che-
hsüeh yü cheng-chih che-hsüeh"). Interpreter
Shih Hu, recorders lectures 1-4 Wang Wu, lectures
5-16 Fu-yüan Sun. [Sixteen lectures delivered in
Peking, sponsored by the National Peking University, the Ministry of Education, the Aspiration
Society, and the New Learning Association.]
 Academic Lamp, 24 Sept. 1919-2 Apr. 1920,
  passim.
 Awakening, 24 Sept. 1919-1 Apr. 1920,
  passim.
 Morning Post, at least the first six
  lectures were published prior to
  15 Nov. 1919.
 Citizen's Gazette, at least one lecture
  published before this newspaper was
  suppressed by the government on 25 Oct.
  1919.
 The New China, I, 5 (15 Oct. 1919)-II,
  7 (15 July 1920), *passim.*
 Bulletin of the Ministry of Education,
  Nov. 1919-June 1920, *passim.*
 New Youth, VII, 1 (1 Dec. 1919), 121-34,
  recorder I-han Kao; VII, 2 (1 Jan.
  1920), 163-82; VII, 3 (1 Feb. 1920),
  117-32; VII, 4 (1 Mar. 1920), 1-15,
  recorder Fu-yüan Sun. [Complete through
  lecture 12.]
 Morning Post Supplement, 16 Feb.-29 Mar.
  1920.
 Five Major Lectures of Dewey, pp. 1-126.
Translations:
a. [Jap.] [Title?] Trans. Yoshio Nagano. In *Dyūi
  no shakai tetsugaku* by Yoshio Nagano.
  Tokyo: Chūwa Shoin, 1949. [pp.?]
  [New edition published by Shunjūsha in
  1959. (pp.?)]

142. "The Social Conception of Specialized Education"
("Chuan-men chiao-yü ti she-hui-kuan"). [Inter-
preter and recorder?] [Delivered at the German
sponsored T'ung Chi School in Shanghai.]

  Academic Lamp, 3 June 1920.
  Awakening, 8 June 1920.

143. "Social Evolution" ("She-hui chin-hua"). [Deliv-
ered at the Y.M.C.A. (Shanghai?).]
  Awakening, 7 June 1920. [Interpreter
  and recorder?]
  Academic Lamp, 9 June 1920. Interpreter
  Po-ming Liu, recorder Hui-an Yao.

144. "Social Factors" ("She-hui chih yao-su"). [Three
lectures concerning society, delivered in Tsinan.]
Lecture I: "Social Factors in Education" ("Chiao-
yü chih she-hui ti yao-su"). [Interpreter and re-
corder?]
  Morning Post Supplement, 24-27 July 1921.
  Awakening, 12 Aug. 1921. Interpreter
  Cho-jan Wang.
  Bulletin of the Ministry of Education,
  Sept. 1921, 7-12.
  Collected Speeches of Dewey and Russell,
  pp. 1-11.
Lecture II: "The Relationship between School Sub-
jects and Society" ("Hsüeh-hsiao k'o-mu yü she-hui
shih kuan-hsi"). [Interpreter and recorder?]
  Morning Post Supplement, 3-7 Aug. 1921.
  Awakening, 18 Aug. 1921. Interpreter
  Cho-jan Wang.
  Bulletin of the Ministry of Education,
  Nov. 1921, 5-7.
  Collected Speeches of Dewey and Russell,
  pp. 11-19.
Lecture III: "The Relationship of School Admin-
istration and Organization with Society" ("Hsüeh-
hsiao ti hsing-cheng ho tsu-chih yü she-hui chih
kuan-hsi"). [Interpreter and recorder?]
  Morning Post Supplement, 8-10 Aug. 1921.
  Awakening, 21 Aug. 1921. Interpreter
  Cho-jan Wang.
  Bulletin of the Ministry of Education,
  Dec. 1921, 33-36.
  Collected Speeches of Dewey and Russell,
  pp. 19-25.

145. "Spontaneity in Learning" ("Tzu-tung ti yen-chiu").
[Interpreter and recorder?] [Delivered at the
Y.M.C.A. in Foochow, Fukien province.]
  Morning Post Supplement, 23 June 1921.

Academic Lamp, 17 July 1921.
Bulletin of the Ministry of Education,
Aug. 1921, 39-40.

146. "Student Government" ("Hsüeh-sheng tsu-chih").
Interpreter Shih Hu, recorders Ju-p'u Liu and
Cheng-hsiang Shao. [A lecture delivered at Peking Teachers' College on its founding day, which
was also the founding day of the student government organization.]
The New Education, II, 2 (Oct. 1919),
163-66.
Democracy and Education, 7 (22 Nov. 1919),
[pp.?].

147. "Three Philosophers of the Modern Period" ("Hsien-
tai ti san ko che-hsüeh chia"). Interpreter Shih
Hu, recorder Fu-yüan Sun. [Six lectures delivered
in Peking.]
Morning Post Supplement, 8-19, 22-27 Mar.
1920.
Academic Lamp, 12, 13, 16-18 Mar. 1920
(James); 9-23 Mar. 1920 (Bergson);
26-31 Mar. 1920 (Russell).
Awakening, 10, 15, 18, 21, 25, 28, 29
Mar. 1920. [Recorder?]
Bulletin of the Ministry of Education,
Apr. 1920, 17-21; May 1920, 15-20;
June 1920, 29-49.
Five Major Lectures of Dewey, pp. 343-98.
Translations:
a. [Jap.] *Gendai sanko tetsugakka*. Trans. and com-
mentary by Yoshio Nagano. Tokyo: Kaizō-
sha, 1934. [pp.?]
b. [Jap.] [Title?] Trans. Yoshio Nagano. In *Gen-
dai obei no tetsugaku* by Yoshio Nagano.
Tokyo: Kaizōsha, 1934. [pp.?]
c. [Jap.] "Gendai sanko tetsugakka." Trans. Yoshio
Nagano. In *Dyūi "kyōiku tetsugaku" no
"gendai sanko tetsugakka"* by Yoshio Nagano.
Tokyo: Shunjūsha, 1951. [pp.?]
2nd printing, 1952

148. "Trends in Elementary Education" ("Hsiao-hsüeh
chiao-yü chih ch'u-shih"). Interpreter Hsiao-
ts'ang Cheng, recorders Tan Ch'en and Ping-k'uei
Shen.
Academic Lamp, 9 July 1920.

149. "Trends in Modern Education" ("Chin-tai chiao-yü chih ch'u-shih"). Interpreter Po-ming Liu, recorder I. Ch'iu.
    Academic Lamp, 13 May 1920.

150. "Trends in Modern Education" ("Hsien-tai chiao-yü ti ch'u-shih"). Interpreter Shih Hu, recorders first and third lectures Han Lu, second lecture T'ien Feng. [Three lectures delivered at the Peking National Academy of Fine Arts.]
    Weekly Critic, 27 (22 June 1919), 1-4.
    The New Education, I, 4 (May 1919), 417-29. [Dated May, but actually published in late June or later.]
    Academic Lamp, 30 June,1, 2 July 1919.
    The New China, I, 3 (15 July 1919), 95-109.
    Educational Tide, I, 3 (Aug. 1919), [pp.?].
    Bulletin of the Ministry of Education, Sept. 1919, 17-18; Oct. 1919, 11-24.
    Awakening, 27 Apr. 1921.
    New Kansu, I, 5 (20 May 1921), [pp.?]. [Incomplete.]
    Collected Speeches of Dewey and Russell, pp. 26-53.

151. "Types of Thinking" ("Ssu-hsiang chih p'ai-pieh"). Interpreter Shih Hu, recorders lectures 1-6 Shao-yü Kuo, lectures 7-8 Fu-yüan Sun. [Eight lectures delivered at the National Peking University.]
    Academic Lamp, 20 Nov. 1919-8 Feb. 1920, *passim*.
    Awakening, 20, 26-27 Nov. 1919; 20-21 Jan. 1920 (lecture 6), recorder Shao-yü Kuo; 2-8, 15-16 Dec. 1919; 31 Jan. 1920 (lecture 7), recorder Fu-yüan Sun.
    Bulletin of the Ministry of Education, Dec. 1919-May 1920, *passim*.
    The New Tide, II, 2 (Dec. 1919)-II, 5 (July 1920), *passim*.
    Five Major Lectures of Dewey, pp. 259-352. Recorder Shao-yü Kuo.
    The New China, II, 3 (15 Mar. 1920)- II, 5 (15 May 1920), *passim*. [Recorder?] [This text is different from all the above versions and is incomplete.]

152. "The University and the Importance of Public
Opinion in a Democracy" ("Ta-hsüeh yü min-chih
kuo yü-lun ti chung-yao"). Interpreter Shih Hu,
recorder Shang-te Kao. [Delivered at the National Peking University on the twenty-second anniversary of its founding.]
> *Morning Post Supplement*, 20 Dec. 1919.
>   [Interpreter and recorder?]
> *The New Tide*, II, 3 (Feb. 1920),
>   591-93.
> *Bulletin of the Ministry of Education*,
>   Feb. 1920, 49-50.

153. "Vocational Education and the Labor Question"
("Chih-yeh chiao-yü yü lao-tung wen-t'i"). [In-
terpreter and recorder?]
> *Awakening*, 31 May 1920.
> *Collected Speeches of Dewey and Russell*,
>   pp. 54-58.

154. "The Work of Educators" ("Chiao-yü-che ti kung-
tso"). [Interpreter and recorder?]
> *Morning Post Supplement*, 22, 23 July 1921.
> *Awakening*, 26 July 1921.

Bibliographical Sources

[From shelf holdings of the libraries of Southern Illinois
University, the University of Illinois at Champaign-Urbana,
and the University of Chicago]

L'Année philosophique, 1890-1913, F. Pillon, ed. Paris:
F. Alcan.
Anuario bibliográfico colombiano, 1951-1963, Ruben Perez
Ortiz, ed. Bogotá: Instituto Caro y Cuervo, Dept. de
Bibliografía.
Anuario bibliográfico costarricense, 1956-1965. San José:
Impr. Nacional.
Anuario bibliográfico cubano, 1940-1960 (Havana); superseded
by *Peraza-bibliografía cubana*, 1961-1965, Fermín Peraza
Sarausa, ed. Gainesville, Fla.: Anuario Bibliográfico
Cubano.
Anuario bibliográfico dominicano, 1944-1945. Ciudad Tru-
jillo: Sección de Canje y Difusión Cultural de la Secre-
taría de Estado de Educación y Bellas Artes.
Anuario bibliográfico peruano, 1943-1960. Lima: Ediciones
de la Biblioteca Nacional.
Anuario bibliográfico puertorriqueño, 1940-1954, G. Valáz-
quez, ed. Río Piedras: Biblioteca de la Universidad.
Anuario bibliográfico salvadoreño, 1952. San Salvador:
Editorial Casa de la Cultura.
Anuario bibliográfico venezolano, 1942-1948. Caracas: Bib-
lioteca Nacional.
Archives de philosophie, 1923-1954. Paris: G. Beauchesne.
The Art Index, Jan. 1929-Jan. 1968. New York: H. W. Wilson
& Co.
*Avviamento alla filosofia, con una piccola guida storico-
bibliografica*, 1950. Armando Carlini, ed. Florence:
G. C. Sansoni.
Barsortiments-Lagerkatalog, 1952-1956. Stuttgart: Koehler
& Volckmar.
Berliner Titeldrucke, fünfjahrs Katalog, 1910-1937, 1955-
1963. Berlin: Staatsbibliothek.
*Biblio: Catalogue des ouvrages parus en langue française
dans le monde entier*, Jan. 1934-July 1967. Paris:
Librairie Hachette.
Bibliografía argentina de artes y letras, 1959-1963. Buenos
Aires: Fondo Nacional de las Artes.

94

Bibliografía brasileira, 1938-1966. Rio de Janeiro: Ministerio de Educação e Cultura; Instituto Nacional do Livro.

Bibliografía Española, 1903-1942; superseded by *Bibliografía Hispana*, 1943-1966. Madrid: Ministerio de Educación Nacional.

Bibliografía filosófica española e hispanoamericana, 1940-1964, Luis Martinez Gómez, ed. Barcelona: Juan Flors.

Bibliografía filosófica del siglo xx, 1952. Buenos Aires: Ediciones Peuser.

Bibliografia filosofica italiana, 1900-1953. Rome: Editora Delfino.

Bibliografía guatemalteca, 1960-1962. Guatemala City: Tipografía Nacional.

Bibliografía hispánica, 1948, 1955-1957; superseded by *El libro español*, 1958-1967. Madrid: Instituto Nacional del Libro Español.

Bibliografia italiana, 1886-1933 (Milan); superseded by *Bibliografia nazionale italiana*, 1958-1967. Florence: Biblioteca Nazionale Centrale di Firenze.

Bibliografia republicii populare romîne, 1956-1967. Bucharest: Biblioteca Centrală de Stat.

Bibliografía Uruguaya, 1946-1949, 1962. Montevideo: Biblioteca del Poder Legislativo.

Bibliografický Katalog, 1922-1950; superseded by *Česke Knihy*, 1951-1967. Prague: National University Library of Prague.

Bibliografie van Afrikaanse Boeke, 1861-1953. Johannesburg: P. J. Nienaber.

Bibliografii I Nauki O Księzce: Bibliographia poloniae bibliographica, 1937-1962. Warsaw: National Library, Bibliographic Institute.

Bibliografua jugoslavue, 1965-1967. Belgrade: Jugoslovenski Bibliografiski Institut.

Bibliographia Anastatica, 1964-1967. Amsterdam: Nieuwe Herengracht.

Bibliographia philosophica, 1934-1945, 1950-1954, G. A. DeBrie, ed. Brussels: Ed. Spectrum.

Bibliographie de Belgique, 1875-1919. Brussels: Bibliothèque Royale.

Bibliographie de la philosophie, 1938-1939, 1946-1953 (Vrin); superseded by *Bulletin trimestrial*, 1954-1963. Paris: International Institute of Philosophy.

Bibliographie der deutschen Rezensionen und Referenen, 1900-1943. Osnabrück: Felix Dietrich.

Bibliographie der deutschen Zeitschriftenliteratur, superseded by *Internationale Bibliographie der Zeitschriftenliteratur*, 1896-1964. Osnabrück: Felix Dietrich.

Bibliographie der Fremdsprachigen Zeitschriftenliteratur, superseded by *Internationale Bibliographie der Zeitschriftenliteratur*, 1911-1964. Osnabrück: Felix Dietrich.

Bibliographie der philosophischen, psychologischen, und pädagogischen Literatur in der deutschsprachigen Schweiz, 1900-1940, 1944. Eugen Heuss, *et al.*, eds. Basel: Verlag für Recht und Gesellschaft.

Bibliographie der Sozialwissenschaften, 1913-1966. Berlin:
Julius Springer.
Bibliographie luxembourgeiose, 1957-1965, Pierre Frieden,
ed. Luxembourg: Bibliothèque Nationale.
Bibliographie nationale suisse, 1896-1911. Bern: K. J.
Wyss.
*Bibliographie; van in Nederland verschenen officiële en
semi-officiële uitgaven,* 1953, 1957-1964. Amsterdam:
Koninklijke Bibliotheek.
Bibliographische Einführungen in das Studium der Philosophie,
1948, I. M. Bochenski, ed. Bern: A. Francke.
*Bibliotheca hispana: Revista de información y orientación
bibliográficas,* 1942-1966. Madrid: Consejo Superior de
Investigaciones Científicas.
Boletín bibliográfico argentino, 1884-1947; superseded by
Boletín bibliográfico nacional, 1950-1953. Buenos Aires:
Ministerio de Educación de la Nación.
Boletín bibliográfico boliviano, 1965-1966, Antonio Paredes
Candía, ed. La Paz: Candía.
Books from Switzerland, 1963, 1965. Zurich: The Swiss
Booksellers' and Publishers' Association.
Brinkman's Cumulatieve Catalogus van Boeken, 1916-1963,
Dirk de Jong, ed. Leiden: A. W. Sijthoff.
British Museum General Catalogue of Printed Books, 1875-
1965. London: British Museum.
The British National Bibliography, 1950-1966. London:
Council of the British National Bibliography.
Bulletin analytique de bibliographie hellénique, 1946-1961.
Athens: Institut Français d'Athènes.
Bulletin signalétique, 1947-1966. Paris: Centre de Docu-
mentation du C.N.R.S.
Catálogo general de la librería española e hispanoamericana,
1901-1930; superseded by *Catálogo general de la librería
española,* 1931-1950. Madrid: Instituto Nacional del
Libro Español.
Catalogo generale della libreria italiana, 1875-1959,
Attilio Pagliaini, ed. Milan: Associazione Italiana
Editori.
Catalogue général de la librairie française, 1840-1925.
Paris: Service Bibliographique Hachette.
*Catalogue général des livres imprimés de la Bibliothèque
Nationale,* 1875-1964. Paris: Bibliothèque Nationale.
Cordier's bibliotheca sinica, 1904-1924, Henry Cordier, ed.
Paris: Guilmoto. Continued by *China in Western Litera-
ture,* 1925-1958, Tung-li Yuan, ed. New Haven, Conn.:
Far Eastern Publications of the Yale University Press.
*Cornell University Library Catalog of the New York State
School of Industrial and Labor Relations,* 1967. Boston:
G. K. Hall and Company.
The John Crerar Library Catalog, 1967. Boston: G. K. Hall
and Company.
Current Caribbean Bibliography, 1954-1961. Port of Spain,
Trinidad: Caribbean Commission, Central Secretariat.
Dania Polyglotta, 1901-1959. Copenhagen: Bibliotheque
Royale.

Dansk bogfortegnelse, 1861-1967. Copenhagen: G. E. C. Gads Forlag.

Decennial Index to Philosophical Literature, 1939-1950. New York: F. Moore Company.

Den ny filosofi, 1963, Justus Hartnack, ed. Copenhagen: Berlingske Forlag.

Deutsche Nationalbibliographie und Bibliographie des im Ausland erschienenen deutschsprachigen Schrifttums, 1958-1967. Leipzig: Verlag für Buch- und Bibliothekswesen.

Diccionario de filosofía, 1958, José Ferrater Mora, ed. Buenos Aires: Ed. Sudamericana.

Dicionário de filosofia, 1952. Orris Soares, ed. Rio de Janeiro: Ministério da Educação e Saúde, Instituto Nacional do Livro.

Diccionario filosófico, 1952. Buenos Aires: Espasa-Calpe.

Dictionaire des philosophes, 1962. Paris: Editions Seghers.

Dizionario di filosofia, 1964, Nicola Abbagnano, ed. Turin: Unione Tipografico.

Enciclopedia filosofica, 1957. Rome: Instituto per la Collaborazione Culturale.

The Encyclopedia of Philosophy, 1967, Paul Edwards, ed. New York: The Macmillan Company.

Fichero: Bibliográfico Hispanoamericano, 1961-1967. Buenos Aires: Bowker Editores.

Handbook of Philosophy, 1959, Michael H. Briggs, ed. New York: Philosophical Library.

Handwörterbuch der Philosophie, 1913 ed., Rudolf Eisler, ed. 1922 ed., Richard Müller, ed. Berlin: Freienfels.

Harvard University Peabody Museum of Archaeology and Ethnology Library, 1963. Boston: G. K. Hall and Company.

Het Boek in Vlaanderen, 1946-1966. Antwerp: Van de Vereeniging ter Bevordering van Het Vlaamsche Boekwegen.

The Hispanic Society of America Library, 1962. Boston: G. K. Hall and Company.

Histoire de la philosophie, métaphysique, philosophie des valeurs; publication entreprise sous les auspices de la UNESCO, 1939-1948. Paris: Hermann.

Index to Latin American Periodical Literature, 1929-1962. Boston: Pan American Union, Columbus Memorial Library.

Index Translationum, 1932-1940 (The League of Nations); 1948-1966. Paris: UNESCO.

Indian National Bibliography, 1957-1968, B. S. Kesavan, ed. Calcutta: Central Reference Library.

Inéditos de filosofia em Portugal, 1949, Manuel G. Costa, ed. Braga: Livraria Cruz.

Instituto nazionale per le relazioni culturali con l'estero, 1920-1941. Rome: I.R.C.E.

International Bibliography of Historical Sciences, 1926-1963. Lausanne: International Committee of Historical Sciences and UNESCO.

International Bibliography of Periodical Literature Covering All Fields of Knowledge, 1965-1967, Otto Zeller, ed. Osnabrück: Felix Dietrich.

International Bibliography of Social and Cultural Anthropology, 1955. Paris: UNESCO.

Inter-American Congress of Philosophy, 1959. Buenos Aires:
Exposición del Libro Americano de Filosofía.
*Jahresbericht über die Erscheinungen der anglo-amerikanischen
Litteratur der Jahre 1894-1895*, Ludwig Busse, ed. Leipzig:
[n.p.].
Jahres Verzeichnis des deutschen Schrifttums, 1945-1956.
Leipzig: Börsenverein.
Journal de l'imprimerie et de la librairie [or] *Bibliographie
de la France*, 1930-1967. Paris: Au Cercle de la Librairie.
The Journal of Unified Science [*Erkenntnis*] 1930-1940,
Rudolf Carnap and Hans Reichenbach, eds. The Hague: W. P.
Van Stockum & Zoon.
Koehler und Volckmar Literatur Katalog, 1952-1967. Stutt-
gart: Koehler and Volckmar.
Leipziger Bücherkatalog, 1960-1967. Leipzig: Deutscher
Buch- Export und- Import G.M.B.H.
La librairie française, 1933-1966. Paris: Au Cercle de la
Librairie.
Library of Congress Catalog, 1942-1946, supplements 1948-
1957, 1958-1962, 1962-1966. Ann Arbor, Mich.: J. W.
Edwards.
Livros de Portugal, 1952-1967. Lisbon: Boletim Mensal do
Grémio Nacional dos Editores e Livreiras.
The London Bibliography of the Social Sciences, 1931-1962.
London: British Library of Political and Economic Science.
Magyar nemzeti bibliográfia; bibliographia Hungarica, 1952-
1967. Budapest: National Széchenyi Library.
Manuel de bibliographie philosophique, 1956, Gilbert Varet,
ed. Paris: Presses Universitaires de France.
Manual del librero hispanoamericano, 1950, Antonio Paulau y
Dulcet, ed. Madrid, Barcelona: Librería Palau.
New York Library Reference Department Slavonic Collection,
1959. Boston: G. K. Hall and Company.
Norsk bokfortegnelse, 1883-1921 (Kristiania); superseded by
Norwegian National Bibliography, 1928-1962. Oslo: Norske
Bokhandlerforening.
*Österreichische Bibliographie; Verzeichnis der österreich-
ischen Neuerscheinungen*, 1957-1967. Vienna: Osterreich-
ischen Nationalbibliotek.
Opera Omnia; Dichter und Denker der Welt in Gesamtausgaten,
1964. Berlin: Werbegemeinschaft Elwert und Meuer.
Pequeño vocabulário da língua filosófica, 1961. São Paulo:
Companhia Editôra Nacional. A translation of *Nouveau
vocabulaire philosophique*, Armand Cuvillier, ed. Trans-
lated by Lólio Laournço de Oliveira and J. B. Damasco
Penna.
*Philosophen-Lexicon; Handwörterbuch der Philosophie nach
Personen*, 1949-1950, compiled and edited by Werner Zeigen-
fuss and Gertrud Jung. Berlin: de Gruyter.
Philosophical Books, 1960-1967. Leicester, England: Lei-
cester University Press.
Philosophie, 1950, Raymond Bayer, ed. Bayeux: R. P. Colas.
*Die Philosophie der Gegenwart; eine Internationale Jahres-
übersicht*, 1908-1915. Heidelberg: Weiss.

Philosophie und Grenzgebiete, 1945-1964. Cologne: Koehler
& Volckmar.
Philosophischer Handkatalog, 1926, Felix Meiner, ed. Leip-
zig: [n.p.].
Philosophisches Wörterbuch, 1951, Walter Brugger, ed. Frei-
burg: Herder.
Philosophisches Wörterbuch, 1922, Paul Thormeyer, ed.
Leipzig: B. G. Teubner.
*Prezewodnik bibliograficzny; urzędowy wykaz druków wydanych
w polskiej rzeczypospolitej ludowej*, 1945-1965. Warsaw:
National Bibliographical Institute.
The Psychological Index, 1895-1936. Princeton, N. J.:
Psychological Review Company.
Quarterly Bulletin of Chinese Bibliography, 1935-1946.
Peiping: National Library of Peiping.
Répertoire bibliographique, 1934-1948; superseded by *Réper-
toire bibliographique de la philosophie*, 1949-1967.
Louvain: Ed. de l'Inst. Supérieur de Philosophie.
Russian Philosophical Terminology, 1964, Karl G. Ballestrem,
ed. Dordrecht, Holland: D. Reidel Publishing Company.
*Schweizer Bücherverzeichnis. Repertoire du livre suisse.
Repertorio del libro svissero*. 1951-1965. Zurich:
Schweizerischer Buchhändler und Verlagerverein. [A tri-
lingual bibliography.]
Schweizerische Landesbibliotek, 1901-1947 (Franke); super-
seded by *Das Schweizer Buch*, 1957-1967. Bern: Benteli.
Scripta recenter edita, 1959-1967. Nijmegen: Bestelcen-
trale der V.S.K.B.
*A Selected Bibliography on Values, Ethics, and Esthetics in
the Behavioral Sciences and Philosophy*, 1920-1958, Ethel
M. Albert, Clyde Kluckhohn, *et al.*, eds. Glencoe, Ill.:
Free Press.
Serie bibliográfica de la Biblioteca Americana de Nicaragua,
1943-1947. Managua: American Library of Nicaragua.
Servicio bibliográfico chileno, 1940-1966. Santiago:
Librería y Editorial Zamorano y Caperan.
Slovenská kniha, 1951-1965. Bratislava: Bibliographical
Institute of the Slovak University Library.
Soupis československé literatury, 1901-1925, Karel Nosovský
and Vilém Pražák, eds. Prague: Nakl. Svazu Knihkupců a
Nakladatelů.
Standard Catalog for Public Libraries, 1932, Minnie Earl
Sears, ed. New York: The H. W. Wilson Company.
Stučný filosofický slovník, 1966. Prague: Svoboda.
Suomessa ilmestyneen kirjallisuuden luettelo, 1945-1966.
Helsinki: Kirjallisuuden Seuran Kirjapainon Oy.
Svensk bok-katalog, 1886-1960. Stockholm: Tidningsaktie-
bolaget Svensk Bokhandel.
Türkiye Tahih Yayinlari Bibliyografyasi, 1729-1950. Ankara:
Milli Egitim Basimevi.
*The United States Department of Health, Education, and Wel-
fare Library Catalog*, 1965. Boston: G. K. Hall and Com-
pany.
University of London School of Oriental and African Studies

Library Catalog, 1963. Boston: G. K. Hall and Company.
Vollstandiges Bücher-Lexicon, 1883-1910 (Tauchnitz), Chris-
tian Gottlob Kayser, ed.; superseded by *Deutsches Bücherverzeichnis*, 1911-1950 (Verlag für Buch- und Bibliotek-
swesen); superseded by *Deutsche Bibliographie: Halb-
jarhres-Verzeichnis*, 1951-1967. Leipzig: Börsenverein
der deutschen Buchhändler.
Wörterbuch der philosophischen Begriffe und Ausdrucke, 1904,
1910, 1927-1930, Rudolf Eisler, ed. Berlin: E. S. Mittler
& Sohn.
Zeitschrift für philosophische Forschung, 1946-1968. Reut-
lingen: Gryphius.

UNIVERSITY LIBRARIES:
  California, University of
  Chicago, University of
  Columbia University
  Cornell University
  Harvard University
  Illinois, University of
  Indiana University
  Iowa State University
  Iowa, State University of
  Johns Hopkins University
  Minnesota, University of
  New York University
  Northwestern University
  Pennsylvania, University of
  Princeton University
  Rutgers University
  Southern California, University of
  Stanford University
  Texas, University of
  Vermont, University of
  Yale University

LIBRARIES AND AGENCIES:
  Universidad Nacional de La Plata, Facultad de Humanidades
    y Ciencias de la Educación, La Plata, Argentina.
  National Library of Australia, Canberra, Australia.
  Österreichische Nationalbibliothek, Vienna, Austria.
  Bibliothèque Royale de Belgique, Brussels, Belgium.
  Instituto Brasileiro de Bibliografia e Documentação,
    Rio de Janeiro, Brazil.
  National Library, "Cyril and Methodius," Sofia, Bulgaria.
  National Library, Public Archives Building, Ottawa, Canada.
  Office of the Registrar of Books and Newspapers, Gangoda-
    wila, Nugegoda, Ceylon.
  National Central Library, Taipei, Taiwan, China.
  Knihovna, Československé Socialistické Republiky,
    Universitní Knihovna, Prague, Czechoslovakia.
  The Royal Library, Copenhagen, Denmark.
  National Library, Cairo, Egypt.
  Kreutzwald-State Library of the Estonian S.S.R., Tallinn,
    Estonia.

Helsinki University Library, Helsinki, Finland.
Pädagogische Zentralbibliothek, Berlin, Germany.
Deutsche Bibliothek, Stiftung des öffentlichen Rechts,
    Frankfurt, Germany.
Comenius-Bücherei, Leipzig, Germany.
Deutsche Bücherei Leipzig, Leipzig, Germany.
Forschungsstelle für vergleichende Erziehungswissenschaft
    der Philipps-Universität Marburg, Marburg, Germany.
Orszagos Pedagogiai Konyvtar, Budapest, Hungary.
Government of India National Library, Calcutta, India.
Centro Nazionale di Informazioni Bibliografiche, Biblio-
    teca Nazionale Centrale Vittorio Emanuele II, Rome,
    Italy.
Central National Library of Korea, Seoul, Korea.
State Library of the Latvian S.S.R., Riga, Latvia.
Lebanese Republic National Library, Beirut, Lebanon.
Biblioteca Nacional, México, D. F., México.
Universiteits-Bibliotheek, Amsterdam, The Netherlands.
General Assembly Library, Parliament House, Wellington,
    New Zealand.
Far Eastern University, Library Department, Manila,
    Philippines.
The National Library, Republic of the Philippines, Depart-
    ment of Education, Manila, Philippines.
The Library of the University of the Philippines, Quezon
    City, Philippines.
Biblioteka Narodowa, Warsaw, Poland.
Biblioteca Nacional de Lisboa, Lisbon, Portugal.
Biblioteca Centrală de Stat, Republica Socialista Romania,
    Bucharest, Romania.
The State Library, Pretoria, South Africa.
Biblioteca Nacional, Servicio Nacional de Información
    Documental y Bibliográfica, Madrid, Spain.
Kungliga Biblioteket, Stockholm, Sweden.
Bibliothèque National Suisse, Service d'Information
    Bibliographique, Bern, Switzerland.
National Library, Bibliographical Institute, Ankara,
    Turkey.
Library of Congress, Reference Department, Washington,
    D.C.
New York State Library, Albany, New York.
United States Information Agency, Washington, D.C.
State Library of the Peoples' Education, Academy of
    Pedagogical Sciences, Moscow, U.S.S.R.
Biblioteca Nacional, Caracas, Venezuela.

Index of Languages

Kannada: *16j*

Korean: *1e, 4l, 5f, 7b,
8r, 8s, 8dd, 8ee, 12d,
14n, 16k, 16u, 21i, 21n,
27g, 28b, 33g, 51j, 51w,
53u, 64c*

Latvian: *53v*

Malayalam· *16l, 51k*

Marathi: *8t, 16m*

Polish: *1f, 1g, 4m, 4n,
8u, 12e, 12f, 20i, 27h,
27i, 35f, 36m, 41a, 53w,
53x, 64d, 64e*

Portuguese: *4o, 4p, 5g,
7c, 8v, 8ff, 8gg, 13h,
16n, 16v, 20j, 20k, 21j,
21o, 26e, 26f, 28c, 31e,
33h, 51l, 51m, 51x*

Punjabi: *13i*

Rumanian: *1h, 1i, 4q, 4r,
12g, 12h, 27j, 27k, 55g,
64b, 64g*

Russian: *1j, 4s, 8hh, 20l,
44d, 53y, 53z, 53aa,
53bb, 54a, 55h, 55i, 55j*

Serbo-Croatian: *8w, 26g,
33d, 53cc*

Spanish: *1k, 1l, 2a, 2b,
3d, 4t, 4u, 4v, 4x, 5d,
6a, 8x, 8ii, 8jj, 8kk,
8ll, 9a, 10a, 11c, 12i,
13j, 14o, 15b, 16o, 16p,
17b, 20m, 20n, 21k, 21p,
21q, 26h, 26i, 27l, 31f,
33e, 36n, 36o, 36p, 36q,
36r, 36s, 36t, 36u, 38a,
42a, 44c, 47a, 49a, 50f,
51n, 51o, 53dd, 53ee,
54b, 55k, 55l, 56a, 58h,
60c, 65*

Swedish: *4w, 4y, 4z, 8mm,
21l, 27m, 53ll, 53mm,
53nn, 53oo, 53pp, 55m,
63c*

Tamil: *16q, 51p*

Turkish: *8y, 16r, 16s, 20o,
29a, 29b, 35g, 53ff, 53gg,
55n*

Urdu: *13e, 13k*

Index of Translators, Editors, Prefacers, Recorders, and Interpreters

Index of Introductions
and Prefaces

Title and Entry Number		Name	Lan- guage
ART AS EXPERIENCE	*3b*	Corrado Maltese	Ital.
	3d	Samuel Ramos	Span.
THE CHILD AND THE *CURRICULUM*	*4h*	P. A. Kleinberger	Hebr.
	4o	Anísio S. Teixeira	Port.
	4t	Lorenzo Luzuriaga	Span.
A COMMON FAITH	*5a*	Guido Calogero	Ital.
DEMOCRACY AND EDUCATION	*8e*	Erich Hylla	Germ.
	8h	Yomtov Helman	Hebr.
	8y	Mehmed Emin	Turk.
[Selection]	*8hh*	S. T. Shatskii	Russ.
[Selection]	*8mm*	Alf Ahlberg	Swed.
EXPERIENCE AND EDUCATION	*14h*	Marie-Anne Carroi	Fren.
	14l	Ernesto Codignola	Ital.
EXPERIENCE AND NATURE	*15b*	José Gaos	Span.
[Selection]	*15d*	Nicola Abbagnano	Ital.
FREEDOM AND CULTURE	*16a*	Amīn Mursī Qandīl	Arab.
	16n	Eustáquio Duarte	Port.
	16o	Angela Romera Vera	Span.
HOW WE THINK	*20f*	Leopold Deuel	Germ.
	20g	Antonio Guccione- Monroy	Ital.
	20i	Zygmunt Myslakowski	Pol.
HUMAN NATURE AND CONDUCT	*21e*	Lamberto Borghi	Ital.
INDIVIDUALISM, OLD AND *NEW*	*23b*	Felice Villani	Ital.
INTEREST AND EFFORT IN *EDUCATION*	*26e*	Anísio S. Teixeira	Port.

Title and Entry Number		Name	Lan-guage
LOGIC: THE THEORY OF INQUIRY			
	33b	Gérard Deledalle	Fren.
	33c	Aldo Visalberghi	Ital.
	33d	Miladin Životić	Serb.
	33e	Eugenio Imaz	Span.
MORAL PRINCIPLES IN EDUCATION	*35d*	Miloslav Skořepa	Czech
"The Need for a Recovery in Philosophy"	*37a*	Lamberto Borghi	Ital.
THE QUEST FOR CERTAINTY	*50c*	Aldo Visalberghi	Ital.
	50f	Eugenio Imaz	Span.
RECONSTRUCTION IN PHILOSOPHY	*51f*	Guido de Ruggiero	Ital.
	51o	Luis Rodríguez Aranda	Span.
THE SCHOOL AND SOCIETY	*53a*	R. Galt	Arab.
	53h	Ludwig Gurlitt	Germ.
	53i	P. A. Kleinberger	Hebr.
	53m	Ernesto Codignola	Ital.
	53s	Seiichi Miyahara	Jap.
	53aa	S. T. Shatskii	Russ.
	53bb	G. A. Luchinskii	Russ.
	53ee	Domingo Barnés	Span.
THE SCHOOL AND THE CHILD	*54b*	Domingo Barnés	Span.
SCHOOLS OF TOMORROW	*55h*	I. I. Gorbunov-Posadov	Russ.
	55j	Lebedev-Polianskii	Russ.
THEORY OF VALUATION	*60a*	Aldo Visalberghi	Ital.
"What I Believe"	*63c*	Alf Ahlberg	Swed.
L'ECOLE ET L'ENFANT	*64*	Edouard Claparède	Fren.
	64b	Maria Teresa Gentile	Ital.
IL MIO CREDO PEDAGOGICO: ANTOLOGIA DEI SCRITTI SULL'EDUCAZIONE	*66*	Lamberto Borghi	Ital.

Index of Terms

[Numbers refer to items not pages.]

NOTE: As this Checklist went to press, a copy of the translation below was received.

FREEDOM AND CULTURE

[Russ.]   *Svoboda i cul'tura*.   Trans. Leonida Mashkovskogo
[with an introd. by R. N. Redliya].   London:
Overseas Publications Interchange, Ltd., 1968.
xxii, 195 pp.